Meditations
From My Sister's Prayer Couch

Book Design by Alex Johnson

ISBN 13
978-1-63132-231-0

Library of Congress Control Number: 2024909316
Cataloging-in-Publication Data is available upon request.

First Edition

Published in the United States of America by ALIVE Book Publishing
an imprint of Advanced Publishing LLC
3200 A Danville Blvd., Suite 204, Alamo, California 94507
alivebookpublishing.com

PRINTED IN THE UNITED STATES OF AMERICA

10 9 8 7 6 5 4 3 2 1

Meditations
From My Sister's Prayer Couch

Damaris Radutiu

Alive Book Publishing

CONTENTS

ACKNOWLEDGMENTS

First, I want to thank my Lord and Savior Jesus Christ for guiding my pen to write, for it is there where my healing started.

I want to thank my parents, my mother, and my father for walking with me, from the very beginning, always loving me through the most difficult of times. They have taught me what true love and perseverance is, and they will forever remain my heroes. Thank you for holding my hands up, in prayer (like Aaron, Moses) when I got tired. Thank you, for never giving up, no matter how hard. I love you more than I can express.

To my children, Adrianne, and Caleb: you have watched your mother go through the valley of the shadow of death, and many, many times you watched me struggle deeply. In my quest for life fulfilled in the traditional way, I have put you through so much. I cannot tell you how sorry I am but at the same time, how grateful. This book, I hope will allow you to see the raw emotions brought on by betrayal, but also the amazing rebirth, the restoration of your mother and of our relationships. I can only hope for more amazing years and time spent together. For this book is first, for you.

I want to thank my siblings: my brother Emanuel (God with us) whose phone calls, visits and hours of fellowship meant so much to me. You are and will remain an example for me.

My sister Ligia, who never gave up on me, seeing me through this difficult and long, way too long process.

She and her husband Beni were for me, a breath of fresh air. Here is one from the "gorgeous" sister-in-law!

I want to thank my brother Ben: his generosity exceeds most and his readiness to help was and will always be so deeply appreciated.

I want to thank my youngest brother David: your family is a true picture-perfect family, and the help and support you gave me throughout this journey, I will treasure, my "I saw you first", baby brother.

I want to thank my brother Chris: the love you have for your family is exemplar, and your help given to me, when in a conundrum to pick paint, created a canvas of beautiful walls. Thank you for coming to my rescue, so many, many times.

For my brother Mike: for your sensitive heart and your passion for justice, I will be forever grateful.

And finally, for my younger sister Dana: your couch sits on the cover of this book. You were my inspiration, for I desired so much to make your move to Atlanta, GA more bearable. Hope you will find yourself in this book, but ultimately hope you will see the tender love of our Creator God, webbed from cover to cover.

I want to send my love and thankfulness to my friend and mentor Dori: Thank you for not tiring to hear me, guide me and teach me how to pray. Our hours of intense prayers and warfare will remain a foundation for me. Thank you, "D".

To my cousin Shy: girl you rock. The trips we took together, the laughter and tears we shared, (well, most were mine) I will always, always, remember.

To my friend Cathy Estrada: I will always treasure our friendship and your encouragement to press on, to allow

God to do His work, in me and ultimately through me. Thank you, sweet friend.

To my sweet friend Emillienne: your calls, your time, your friendship, and your spirit, were and are for me a reminder that love transcends family relationships and I know we will remain soul sisters for life. Thank you.

To my pastor from the Romanian Church, Ovidiu and his wife Fabi: our friendship endured the test of time. Thank you for walking with me through this long and arduous journey and thank you for your support.

To my friend Cora: girl, you did not give up on me, and you were one of the few who still sent messages, when I checked out for a long time. Your perseverance led me to my church, New Life, and for that I will be forever grateful.

To my many godly women from my church: Josie, Barbara, Cindy Levy, Terry, Edyta, Brenda, Judy and so many others. Thank you for the bottom of my heart.

And to my publisher, Alive Book Publishing: thank you for taking a chance with this book and working to make it see the light of press. Thank you for your helpful inputs and loving guidance. And thank you to my book editor for your tireless work.

Let the words of my mouth and the meditation of my heart be acceptable in your sight, O Lord, my rock and my redeemer. Psalm 19:14 ESV

THE BEGINNING

A Little Boy Named Dana

Walking onto the plane to Atlanta with Georgia on my mind, I was looking for my seat. When my sister Dana purchased the ticket, she had asked me, "Window, middle, or aisle seat?"

"Aisle please," I had replied. "I need to be able to stretch my legs."

Walking towards the back of the plane I found my seat, and just as I was ready to sit down, a gentleman, tapped me on my back.

"Excuse me, " he said. "Could you please switch seats with me? I'd like to sit next to my wife."

"Of course," I said. "Gladly!" Then I turned to look at a very beautiful blonde, blue-eyed mother sitting with an equally beautiful young girl and asked, "May I sit next to you?"

"Sure," came the answer.

I got comfortable and turned to meet the two people who would be my neighbors for the next six hours.

"I'm Kelley," she said. "And this is my daughter, Eva. So nice to meet you."

"I'm Damaris," I replied. "But they call me Demi for short."

As the plane started to take off, I knew immediately that it would be a nice ride. She was so friendly, and Eva looked like a little doll. On the tray in front of her were her toys—a few dolls, some stuffed animals, some children's books, and most importantly, her mom's phone, of course. Children are now born holding a device in their tiny hands. I once heard a comedian say that he was so Japanese he was born cordless. Quite funny, but also true.

As we started to ascend into the air and all through the flight, Eva played with many of her things, but always went back to watching a movie. So sweet! It made me wonder what is popular with kids nowadays. Classics like *The Lion King, Beauty and the Beast, Snow White, Marlin* and *Dory* trying to find his son in *Finding Nemo,* and *Shrek,* were popular when my children were little.

Kelley told me that she lives in the Bay Area but was going to Atlanta where she is originally from to visit her family—her parents and her sisters.

"Why did you choose to live in the Bay Area," I asked?

"My husband, Thomas, and I work here," she told me. "I am going back for two weeks and Thomas will be joining us for the second week."

"Is Eva your only child?" I inquired.

"Yes, she is right now. . ." I heard some hesitation in her voice.

Lord, will she feel comfortable sharing her story with me? Because we ALL have one, don't we, Lord? Because this is how you work in us our sanctification. Yes it is!

After chatting for awhile, I got to meet Kelley on a deeper level. Her parents divorced when she was a teen and apparently her mother wanted the divorce.

"I heard myself utter, "In my case it was my father." Ah! The ugly "D" word rearing its head yet again.

Her parents then married another couple's spouses whom they were friends with. After hearing that, I decided that nothing will shock me anymore. She went on to tell me that she was a swimmer and a lifeguard which I could tell because her beautiful body had the shape of a performance swimmer. She is currently managing a swim club in Palo Alto and recently moved to Fremont.

Her little baby doll is four and a half. I looked at her again and thought, "She will break many hearts," which is what many people say when someone is way too beautiful. Kelley explained that a few years back she was pregnant with twins. I can't even imagine how they must have felt when they found out they were going to have two babies. Apparently, they have many in her family.

But then, right in the middle of her second trimester, she started having problems, including bleeding—every pregnant woman's worse nightmare, because it threatens the life of the beloved inside. And as feared, at twenty weeks, the worst happened. Her heart was going to be tried and broken because God had decided to write a return label on that package.

Her husband was not around at that moment so one of the employees took her to the hospital. What followed next was I am sure one of the most painful experiences a woman and mother has to walk through—she had to give birth to two stillborn babies.

As I write, my sweet sister, Dana, my heart is so heavy for her loss. I can't imagine though I try. Unless you walk in someone's shoes . . . But Lord, you don't make mistakes. The baby girl died in her womb. Then just a few minutes past midnight, the little boy came into this world. But he didn't live very long—only around ten minutes. "He took a few breaths," she said, not holding back tears.

And I thought he probably encountered this sin-infested,

plagued-by-problems earthly air, and his little lungs said, "Nope. Not going to put this in my body. We are going back to the amazing place we came from—heaven! Sorry Mom and Dad, but we will see you there. My sister is waiting, but mostly Jesus is. Until we meet again . . ."

They named her Andie and named him Dana. It was the name of one of Kelley's employees, the instructor who drove her to the hospital. "In his honor," she said, wiping her beautiful blues with a tissue. "In his memory." I'm sure what followed next was a blur—footprints, small caskets, a graveside memorial.

"Where Oh death is your victory? Where Oh death is your sting?" laments Paul in 1 Corinthians 15:55 . . . but thanks be to God, who gives us the victory [as conquerors] through our Lord Jesus Christ." And only by His victory and grace could Kelley and Thomas withstand and overcome the pain, the loss, the questions.

They just celebrated the one-year anniversary of their twins' departure. "We will try again," she said. "I am trying to convince Thomas to have two more."

"So courageous, faithful, strong, and children-loving," I thought. I was sitting next to a saint, an amazing daughter of the King of kings and Lord of Lords. And surely, God must be loving and honoring Kelley.

"I am so sure God will give you more children because He knows your heart and desires, yours and your husband's," I told her.

As we said goodbye after landing in Atlanta, I could not help but wonder again and again at the loving King and amazing God we serve, Dana. Because by His divine appointment, I got to "meet" your namesake in the form of a tiny, sweet, innocent baby boy.

And as I was walking to the baggage claim, I looked up to heaven and whispered, "Can't wait to meet both of you angels."

Until then, shalom.

P.S. I had her permission to share a small part of her life.

Good Night New Mexico

La România se zice una calda și una rece (translation for my American friends: One hot one, one cold one).

As good as yesterday was, today started out promising as well. Though I woke up with a flare-up of my Meniere's disease, I pushed past it and decided to do some stuff—a few more errands. It's so good Dana, to feel "normal "and to not feel that I don't belong, and to be able to look people in the eyes and feel confident that I have something to say that they would be interested in.

I carried on an interesting chat with Jason, a cashier at T.J. Maxx. It felt so good to share with him, even so briefly, my experience in the Holy Land. Oh, the joy of being able to make sense, to not feel defeated by fear. But make no mistake, it tries to overcome me every single day. That is why I thought for my tattoo I would write: Overcomer.

The day was covered in quips about life with my daughter. But with my son, well he had to argue and prove to me over and over that I am wrong and he is right. Caleb knew that we were going to church tonight at 8 p.m. for rehearsal. He knew we were picking up Fabi at Nordies and driving with her. He knew that we were supposed to leave our house at 7:45 p.m. I was ready, but he was not.

"I have to eat," he said. "I'm hungry!"

"Well, grab something to go and let's go!" I replied.

"No. I'm going to warm up chicken and rice and eat that." Not only did he do that, but he took the time to measure all the grams because this is how his life is structured, no matter if it rains or shines. So I was not happy.

"I'd like to get there on time, she is waiting for us," I said.

"Call and tell her we'll be late," he replied.

"No, Caleb, I don't have a good enough excuse."

Going to make the story short:

"Mom, I don't like that you pressure me to sing in church." Say what? I did not do that. I've expressed my desire to have him sing since he has such a beautiful voice and he accepted.

"In fact, I don't think it's right to sing next to such a "difficult" mother. It would not be right."

What? Hold the phone and call Jesus. What in the world? Oh, I remember, we are in a constant battle with the enemy of our souls. How could I have forgotten? Don't you think Damaris (I was talking to myself), that he (the enemy), is mad that you've escaped his traps? That he does not have you under his oppression anymore? Don't you think? I got mad.

"Listen," I said. "This is between you and the Lord. And I'm not going carry this guilt on my shoulders, Bozo. No sir . . . this one is on you. Please don't come," and I left! My heart was crushed yet again.

Dana, you might say, well if he is not right in his hear about it, then he should not sing. And you are right for a bit of it. How about use your talent and give him thanks? Oh, Dana! How much I would have loved to hear him sing. But as I was driving away, the words of the song "I love the Lord" played in my ears and head. Yes . . . he's heard my cry, and the tears started flowing. Tears of regret, tears of disappointment, but also tears of joy for a love so pure for the Master of the universe who is leaning His ear to hear the anguished cry from the one He calls His beloved!

Spring is in the air! And I will rest in the goodness of a carrying Savior. He is the only one who knows fully and who loves with abandon. And He whispered to me as he did so many other times: "Come to me, and I will give you rest! For my yolk is easy and my burden light."

Good night, my darling sister. He is our Lord and only He deserves our whole heart and love. And good night, New Mexico.

Where You Lead Me, I Will Follow

On the plane back from Portland, I tried to get comfortable. Hazel was so agitated in her travel bag, scratching non-stop. Lord, I need her to come down. I started to pray. I took her in my lap and covered her with my long black duster. Surely, she will come down. Nothing!

I knew I had to hide her from the flight attendant. She already told me the carry-on needs to stay under the seat. Lord, she constantly wanted to move, to get off. Okay, let's see what she wants. Thank God the lights in the plane were turned to dim. Love traveling at night. I really do. I tried giving her water. Nothing! Finally, she crossed over onto the window seat, turned on her side, and went to sleep.

Of course! She does this at home. She has no idea we are at ten thousand feet in the air and she just wanted to go to sleep. My sweet fifteen-year-old beautiful Hazel. How I loved her! I covered her with my coat, put the tray from the middle seat up, and put my water and vegetables on it. It was the Lord who arranged for me to have a whole row for myself. Finally, I could relax. Phew!

My dear sister, it was only then that I read your text. Looking at your beautiful handwriting, you always had such good penmanship. Always. I tried to read all the pages. Seven in total, I think, but I could not finish. Sobs came out. Sobs, sob, sobs. Lord, her too? Could she not have been spared? Was she not the most devoted wife and mother? Did she not follow her husband everywhere he wanted to go? From home to home, from America back to Romania, then back to America. A new home. Lived in a trailer. Home was so beautiful. Sold yet again two years later.

"Are you okay with this?" I asked her.

"No," but I'm trying to understand, to be supportive."

Wow. I don't know how and where she gets her strength from. Well, I do. I believe that it was only by His goodness and mercy that she carried on through this move . . . this change. And now she lives in Georgia. Her husband took her away . . . again, clear across the country because he wants land and another house. The effort they did was unimaginable. Back and forth. Moving again after they stayed in a rental for one year. How much more, I wondered, could she take?

And the answer came tonight, on the plane back home. I was allowed to be privy to her soul. Lord, I don't understand. Well, there are so many things I do not understand. What was this weekend about? What happened to Beni? Who is he? I don't recognize him.

But back to my sister. Dani is unhappy? Really? Isn't this what he wanted? No? Again? Why? When and where would he finally find happiness? She said they argued.

Them? He seems to be very loving and devoted. Guess appearances are deceiving. He threatened to leave her? What? Again, what? If she is not the most perfect wife, I don't know any more who is.

Lord? You took her from me, and from Mom and Dad. And I believed all this time and I still do that there is something in Georgia for them . . . for her. But not this. Not this! Visiting Dori on this trip was the highlight of these past three days. Divine appointment. God's providence. His plan. To allow me to reconnect with her four years later. I thought our friendship was forever done. After all, she told me I *had* to stop putting Nick on the throne of my life because that place belongs only to one, and it ain't Nick!

Well, I could not listen. I tried, but failed. And with my failure came the demise of an amazing friendship. Or so I thought! Because today back in her amazing home, the spirit of God gave us a Rhema, a glimpse of heaven. Because there, in her beautiful living room overlooking the Columbia River, we worshiped the King, the only one who loves us unconditionally. Dana, you know what I am saying? This statement is true for so many daughters: Ligia, Dori, Damaris, Dana, Emilliene, Shy, and the list can surely continue.

Oh, looking at the above names, I noticed again: The three "D"s. Remember? Of course, you do! Us, going undercover. The Lord is so good to bring to my remembrance good things from the past.

Dana, He is at work in you. Praise him! Damaris, He is at work in you, let Him! Dori, He is at work in you, impart Him! Ligia, He is at work in you, trust Him! Because as I land in Oakland tonight my heart, after it cried until tears dried, felt a new kind of rhythm, one that surrendered and sings the stanza to the very well-known hymn "Where He Leads Me." And I (we) will follow.

The Goodness of God

I have spent today in a very unique way. I had a desire to call Annabelle. She responded quickly, saying she was working at the restaurant Sideboard in Lafayette. I looked at the clock—it was 10:30.

I called Sideboard and asked, "Do you still serve breakfast?

"Until two," came the answer.

"I'll be there shortly," I replied.

I have been inside this hip cafe restaurant a few times, but never did I take the time to look—to really take it in. Totally amazing decor, combining new with old. I think it's called shabby chic.

She was the hostess taking orders. Saw her beautiful face behind the counter and I wanted to tell the women in front of me: "She my niece! Is she real perty or what?" Now imagine me saying that with a black slang . . . I don't know why but I love to talk like them . . . Hmmmm.

The breakfast was simply the most delicious I've had in a while. I think it's going to be my new "go to" restaurant. She came and sat with me for a little bit during her lunch break and I asked her, "Do you have plans for dinner? Do you want to hang with me?"

She said, "I get off at five and I don't have any plans. I would love to spend some time with you."

As my nail appointment took a little longer than I thought, she got off work early and walked over to the house. She just sat out on the deck, enjoying the sun. When I called to tell her I was coming, she said, "I will meet you down at the bottom of the hill." Together we went to the business to pick up the dogs and I had a bit of work to do. She was so gracious to all the people there, shaking hands and talking to all of my sweet old ladies. She even talked to Nick. I don't know what about because I was busy in the back. After about an hour and a half, we took all three dogs and came home. We ordered sushi and in the privacy of my home, in the beautiful living room surrounded by beautiful doggies, we sat and ate dinner and we watched a movie. We had such a good time.

Before we picked up dinner, I sat at the piano and played a song for her. She was singing along with me and I invited her to join in. We harmonized so well together, I recorded it. I'm pretty sure my parents will be happy to hear that I'm singing again and that she does to.

The food was great and the movie was hilarious. Afterwards, she said to me, "Do you think I can spend the night here since I have to return back to work at 7 a.m.?"

"I would be delighted," I said. "Let's go get your clothes."

After we came home, she took a shower and we sat together outside on the deck, truly admiring God's creation and experiencing His goodness. The song that we listened to and then we recorded, is called "The goodness of God."

He really is so good, Dana! I've spent a lot of time talking to her, and allowing her to talk and share her struggles with alcohol and with some drugs. I looked at a pretty face and I saw so much confusion, so much hurt.

"Lord," I prayed. "You love her so much. Thank you for bringing her into my home and allowing me a small glimpse into her life—tumultuous, with highs and lows. Yet somehow, she felt confident and comfortable to share it with me while smoking her weed.

I have learned a lot from just talking to my beautiful niece, because what I will remember forever is God's amazing goodness. Dana, God is good!

I'm going to retire to bed soon so I can wake up in the morning and praise Him. Good night Leleu family. You are being missed terribly.

Today I learned About Standing Firm in Faith

It is no secret that the devil will try to knock us back from our stance of faith, when we are facing difficult challenges. In James 1:6 we read: "But let him ask in faith, nothing wavering. For he that wavereth is like a wave of the sea driven with the wind and tossed."

We have a crucial choice to make: We can give up, or we can stand our ground and boldly declare: I refuse to be moved off my position of faith because the Word of God is true, and I'm not going to back off. And for us to experience a breakthrough regarding a difficult situation we struggled with, for a long time, we must take a bold stance of faith and say: I will stand. Because it may take time for our answer to manifest. Remember, there is a devil out there who doesn't want us to experience God's will and we also have our flesh to deal with. But faith doesn't vacillate, and it never moves. Faith stands still in one spot. Amen. Glory Hallelujah.

The word "ask," in James chapter one, in Greek, gives the connotation of being firm or adamant in requesting, and I like this. Depicts a person who speaks up, speaks out boldly, and authoritatively. Say what? A person who talks a lot?

Then the next word is in faith, denoting, someone who is praying from a stable immovable position. Faith stands still, and it doesn't waiver.

Third, the verse says that we must ask in faith and don't doubt. In Greek, the word means to differ, or to be at variance with oneself. In other words, our mouths may be saying all the right words, but our hearts are not really in agreement. Until our hearts and minds get into agreement, we are not really asking in faith.

Fourth, James said that if we are not asking in faith, we are like a wave of the sea being tossed and from. The idea here is, that waves may look impressive, but they don't last long. And likewise, a person who doesn't stand firm in faith may temporarily sound impressive when he prays, but is like a wave of the sea, and his prayers and desires are ever-changing. And therefore, he is not standing firm in a position where he can be blessed.

My brother, I sent this to you this morning as an encouragement. I will take this for myself as well, as I acknowledge how many times my faith was wavering. And I'm making a decision to not be a double-minded person, but rather to stand firm in my position of faith until my answer and reward will be fully manifested. I pray you join me on this quest.

Have a great day at work. Will talk soon.

Written to my dear brother Emmanuel, and inspired from the marvelous work of Rick Renner

Follow Peace with All Men, and Holiness, without Which No Man Shall See the Lord. (Hebrews 12 :14)

Reading from my morning devotional, I came across this question: "Do you have a difficult relationship in your life, poisoned by offense, bitterness or misunderstanding?" (Oh boy, do I!)

"It doesn't matter who it is; it could be your spouse, your sibling, your child, your parent, your friend, and so on. The Scripture clearly tells us to follow peace with all men. That includes the list above!"

Because the author is a Greek scholar, he gives new emphasis on the word "follow." In Greek, the world is *diakos*, and it refers to an old hunting term that meant to follow the tracks of an animal, the scent of an animal, and to look and search for that animal until you finally get your prey. Remember, this refers to a hunter (thus the idea of a wounded animal is described here).

The idea, I guess, is that when you have to follow peace, you are to search for it until you find it. You are not to stop until you reach that goal—to track it down because peace doesn't just come to us. So we have to do something to find peace with people, no matter how difficult a particular relationship is, God is telling us that it is our responsibility to try to mend it.

Though we are *not* responsible for what the other person does, we *are* responsible for what we do! Of course, sometimes we do everything we can, but the person doesn't respond. We cannot answer for the other person's attitude, but we are going to have to answer for ourselves.

I struggle and have been struggling to find peace over what happened in my life, especially in the past year or so. So many things that I never thought I would go through. Divorce brought so much craziness. I never would've dreamed in a million years that something this crazy would happen to me. To us. Never! Nothing prepared me for it! But it seems that God is trying to catch my attention this morning, saying: "Follow the tracks of peace," because the Bible goes on to tell us that the reason we are to follow peace with all men is that, "Without it no man shall see the Lord." Hebrews 12:14b.

The world sees and tells us that "lack of peace serves as a blocker and stops us from experiencing the presence of God. And it goes even deeper to say that we are to follow "after holiness," and that we are called to a higher standard. But we cannot do it without the presence of the Holy Spirit living in us and giving us the power to walk in forgiveness.

We are called to walk in holiness. We are called to follow after peace. We are called to walk free from offense. Otherwise, we will remain in a life filled with strife and bitterness, and we won't be really able to experience the tangible presence of God. All good. All understood in my mind. But there's a long road for this to travel from my head to my heart. Yes, there is.

Like my friend Cindy used to say: "Sanctification happens in small bites." As long as we move forward, one small step at a time, victory is ours guaranteed through Him, and only through Him. Putting boots on the ground rather than just living in a theologically sound and filled with knowledge life is what living a Christian life at this time in history means.

I pray that the Holy Spirit will lead me and show me what path to take in this pursuit so I can please the Lord by walking filled with the Holy Spirit. That is the desire of my heart and my prayer I lift to the throne of grace this morning. I will end with a poem I wrote years ago called "Holiness."

I read in Your word that I am holy,
Sanctified, put aside, a special vessel indeed.
Why is this so hard to believe, oh Father?
Is it because I live every day,
Surrounded by sin?

Surely not by deeds, but by faith,
I can fathom,
The holiness that You bestow upon me.
They then, so I listen to the enemy's voices:
You are holy?
Pot of clay, look at you!
Can't you see?

Holy is God, we all know that,
And tremble!
But you?
Look again!
You're just making me laugh!
Enough!
I will not listen to your lies any longer!
He says I am holy!
I am!
So, just stop!

He says if I stay in His word,
If I listen,
His holiness will reflect upon me,
Like a mirror reflects the image of a vessel,
Standing face to face with it,
Perfectly!

I want to live my life out, in victory.
I am holy!
Oh, Father, please help me believe!
Through and through, sanctified,
Put aside and devoted,
To be used by You, dear God,
Exclusively!

Empower me daily,
To live and be ready,
To share this with all who will listen,
Because You say I am holy because YOU are holy!
Oh, vessel of clay,
Believe and rejoice!

A Different Kind of Story

My sweet sister, today I have a different story to tell you, a story that brought so much joy to my life. Started the day with a family conference—me and Nick and the kids. There has been a lot of tension among us. Actually, mostly between Caleb and the three of us. A lot!!! So the "talking stick" was passed around the table and everybody spoke their hearts out. It was beautiful, Dana, to see that as I was praying under my breath, the heavens took notice. A lot was shared, and as I would like to believe for a moment, walls were broken down. I know there is a whole lot of work that needs to be done in each of our lives, but something beautiful has been started.

Last night I had a one-on-one talk with Caleb, Dana, and for the first time, I've seen into his soul. Penetrating beyond the tough exterior, I saw a broken heart hurt by so many people—me, his dad, girls that he's fallen for—and life in general. I loved my broken son in those moments, Dana, the way I have not loved him before. I loved him in the spirit. Does this make sense to you? Do you understand? I don't think I can share this with anyone else.

After our talk, Adrianne and I ran some errands and then went to downtown Walnut Creek. I have not been there for years, Dana. Only three months , I could not enter a store because I was that fearful, and today we returned things at Athleta, and she tried on and bought two cute outfits. We had not done this in so long, I had forgotten the feeling. Then she said, "Mom, I'm hungry," and we had one of the best lunches ever at a Thai restaurant! What do you say to this? Isn't God good? I enjoyed every moment and every bite.

Afterwards I went home, took the doggies, and went over to the business. I solved some minor issues there and talked to my lovely residents, after which I had to run over to CVS. I felt so exhausted, I said to myself, "I'll just rest on the couch for a few minutes and go." But heaven had a different plan. There, held in the sweet arms of the creator of sleep, I fell into one of the most restful naps I've had in a long time—two hours. Say what? I, the person who struggles to sleep, napped for two hours? I guess God who enjoyed our outing and LAUGHED with us saw how tired my body was and said, "Rest for a while my daughter—CVS can wait."

I woke up so refreshed I didn't know what to do with my energy. All my doggies had slept with me as well. So I went to CVS, bought flowers from Trader Joe's, and tomorrow I'll make a nice arrangement. Came home close to 10 p.m. and cooked BBQ chicken breast with plain rice and veggies for Caleb. And now as I'm writing this, my heart is full, Dana. Full of gratitude for a God who in the middle of our crazy, busy, lives, schedules some fun, too. He loves us that much!!!

BTW, We picked up our art. It looks really good! And I also bought myself some L'Occitane body soap which in the past has always filled my whole room with an amazing fragrance. Going to clean the kitchen and then wash up and go to bed. Now this is what I'll call a small slice of heaven.

Rest well, and stay hard-working, God-loving, and always honoring family.

I love you.

HAPPY VALLEY HOME FOR OUR PARENTS

Goodbye, Franco Sarto

I'm staring at the closed door. Tonight, it's my turn to be the night supervisor at the care home. It's almost morning; I slept on and off for only a few hours. But ever since I made my bed on the couch in their living room, the closed door has stared back at me, because behind it sits an empty bed. Empty.

I came back from Portland late Monday night. All weekend I called to check on him. "Is he okay? I asked.

"The same," they said.

Then I got a text from Cathy. "Demi, he has the death rattle!"

No! He can't die without me! I promised him I'd be there—to make it easy.

"Demi?"

"Yes, Frank?"

"I want to die!" he would tell me countless times.

"Well, He is not ready to have you yet!" I would answer, but at ninety-seven, I think he's earned the right to say, "I am done!" I calmed myself when again I was reassured that he was fine, as fine as he could be on hospice.

"The family is exaggerating, Nick said. "You know they are ready for him to pass."

Tuesday morning I got up and there was to a text from Nick. "I left for a few days. A short list of things to do."

Boom. He was gone! So this is how it's going to be. Well, that's okay. I pray that it will end soon!

Walking out of my garage, my neighbor Art met me and said, "Demi, we are blocked! A huge tree fell this morning across our driveway. Didn't you hear the noise?"

"No," I said, thanking God for allowing this to happen this morning and not during the night at 1:00 a.m. when I got home from the airport. God's care on display again. Thank you, Lord. The tree was on our property but it blocked the access to their house which was a bit higher up than ours.

"Oh no! I need to go see Frank," I exclaimed. "But it's okay, I'll walk!"

"Did you forget that you are still very short of breath?" came a voice. "Take an Uber!"

"Yes, of course." Art was so nice.

"Nick is not home," I told him. He has heard this many times before. "He is busy living his life with his mistress. Would you please call a company to help?" I asked.

"I'll take care of it, Demi," he replied. "I'll do the best I can to clear the way. Ann is at work and I hope to have it done by the time she gets home."

"God bless you, Art," I said as I got into the Uber.

Frank was not well. I saw it the second I walked in his room. He did have the rattle. "No more food," I told the caregivers. "None." I called Cathy and Jan, his darling wife. "The end is near," I said. "Please come."

Cat was in Tahoe. "I'm on my way," she said. "Hope she makes it on time," I thought to myself.

Holding Jan, Frank's wife, I listened to her, reminisce. "He was such a gentle giant," she said. "Such a loving husband, father, and grandfather."

I knew that. The pictures on his wall spoke volumes. Around 3:30 I said to Jan: "It's time for morphine," and amazingly, he responded to me.

"Frank?"

"Yes."

"I'm here."

"Yes."

"It's Demi."

"Yes."

"And Jan."

"Yes."

"I'm going to give you something inside your cheek to help you breathe better."

"Yes."

"Could you please try to swallow?"

"Yes," and he did swallow. Oh Lord, thank you for allowing me the privilege.

Slowly, after a few doses, his breathing started to relax. Phil, his son, and Caitlyn, his niece, were around his bed with me and Jan. I watched his body change color.

"He's leaving us, "I told them, and with tears flowing, I started to sing:

"Amazing grace how sweet the sound, that saved a wretch like me . . ." Then Caitlyn joined in. Her voice , so beautiful.

I said, "Let's repeat," as I started to record it. Harmonizing, our voices were full of emotions, hers probably more, because her gentle, loving giant of a grandfather was passing into eternity.

"I once was lost, but now I'm found. Was blind, but now I see."

During this stanza, Frank took his last breath. Aghhh . . .

Aghhh . . . Aghhh . . . straight into the presence of Jesus. "He is gone," I said to his wife. More tears.

"He is not in pain anymore," she whispered softly as she held onto his limp hand. Oh how I wanted to take her pain away, because his was gone, but hers was just beginning. Cat didn't make it on time. Neither did the rest of the family. It didn't matter anymore. "For you are dust, and to dust you shall return," resounds the curse from the garden. Genesis 3:19. Yes, but his spirit, I am fully convinced, went to be with the Lord.

Until we meet again Franco Sarto. Until we meet again! I will never forget you, because you and your darling family left such an imprint in my heart. Until we meet again— in glory.

Under the Fig Tree

Sitting outside on a very beautiful chaise lounge, my eyes are fixed on the fig tree leaves and fruit right above me. Dancing in the slight wind, they seem to want to talk to me, and I entertain the idea. It's been a long ride has it not? I ask as if they could answer. It really has been—many amazing years but also hard years, and you have been privy to all. You have seen and heard so much. You know . . .

Remember when right under your foliage sat gentle ladies and gentlemen who were just enjoying a lazy afternoon? A refreshing drink in the garden? Remember those times? And remember when the gentle giant of a man, Frank, was right inside this room and always watching and admiring you? He sure thought you were majestic.

You have offered juicy amazing fruit to so many for so

many years. You fed us well. And as to not be forgotten, the other trees from the garden rustled: Forgot about us? No, of course I have not. How can I forget the apples and the pears we've collected over the years, the wild plums and the yellow plums, the oranges and the apricots? The raised beds which once were filled with tomatoes and zucchini? Lettuce and green onions?

Lord, this land gave such amazing blessings for me and my family. How do I let it go? Tears wash my face. How to I say goodbye to my home? How do *I let go*? My eyes turned to the roses fragrantly moving in the wind. So many colors and so, so, beautiful.

After a while, my mind goes inside the house, and I could probably walk through each room and hear the voices, the cries, and the laughter of so many who lived here through the last twenty-five years. A house where the love of Christ was manifested by the care given to the ones who chose to allow us the privilege.

How can I not remember big John and little John? Lorie and Anna? Carolyne and Sam? Edith and Alvin? Norma and Dr. Kang? Allison and Mary? Julie and Joyce? Pat and Edna? Joy and Dorothy? Carolyn and Barbara? Frank and Richard?

Ah . . . there will have to be many pages filled with these names, behind the people who will not be forgotten by me. No, I cannot and I will not forget. I gave myself to this and I did it with such passion, so, will treasure them. I will remember the dancing and the singing, the good food served, and the needs covered. But also, the agonizing sounds of rattled breathing and oxygen machines, the comforting hand and the medications that took away their pain as they entered into eternity.

Yes, I was called to be close to the dying. For to be there

put it all in perspective for me personally. I knew that we would all traverse that road and would have to enter into the eternal dimensions. And I was happy to tell whoever was willing to listen that Jesus was the only way to the truth and the light. And I will never forget, when holding Frank's hand and singing the very well-known song, "Amazing Grace," he slipped into eternity. No, I will never forget that, nor will I forget his darling family.

The fig trees can testify of years well spent and well lived under all the circumstances. Maybe one day I will get to reminisce with many of the named above about the goodness of God while living on this sin infected world. About His mercies renewed for all every single day, and about the opportunity to be in each other's lives while living in the beautiful home in the hills of Lafayette.

Goodbye Walnut Lane. Goodbye Happy Valley home. You have a piece of my heart!

Here Today, Gone Tomorrow
—In Memoriam—RB

As I ponder at the meaning of life, so many thoughts invade my mind. What is life? How long is it? Why are we here, and where are we going? Who created us? Does one believe in a Creator God who gave us life and who, according to Scriptures, knows the day we are born and the day we die?

Psalm 139 states: Every day of our lives was written in His book before we were even born, when we were woven together in our mother's womb, He saw us.

I know some of these questions are rhetorical. If anyone

finds the meaning of them, and the answer to them, they find the true sense, the true meaning of what this existence we call life, is.

I was blessed to be given a tender heart towards older people, the elderly who in their advanced age need assistance and help. I was told that it is easy for me because I am a nurse and in many ways, it's true. But it goes beyond the profession and the knowledge. I truly love old people, and I do feel it is my calling to care for them.

I have also been blessed to have this beautiful home that I always jokingly called a five-star hotel for the elderly. For the past twenty-five years many sweet, amazing, beautiful ladies and gentlemen have walked into our home and walked out, into eternity.

Recently, as the body of one of my sweet, sweet residents called Frank was picked up, the ladies that came to pick him up said to me, "You have a very hard job."

And I said, "No, I don't. Because when you love what you do, it's not really a job, it's a passion."

I have collected memories of so many of them through the years, and every once in a while I remember some of them, though of course, some more than others. Such is life.

Sometimes the bond we formed is so deep and strong, it cannot be broken by death. At least I know that is true for me. I could name many names like Frank T. He was an amazing teddy bear giant of a man with a huge heart, who left a big hole in mine. He and his family were simply amazing people whom I will never ever forget.

Yesterday we lost Richard, and as I write these thoughts down, my eyes well up with tears; I cannot see to type . . . I still can't really deal with the reality of him being gone. My sweet, sweet Richard. He was such an amazing man.

So accommodating, never asking for anything even when asked, because he never wanted to bother anyone. And he never complained—never. I really think he was totally content with where he lived because he loved his wife Barbara and he loved us. Their lives, and by intention his life, was simple.

He enjoyed reading the paper, watching TV, sitting in the garden, and eating good food. He enjoyed sweet little Zoe, who every time she entered the house ran straight up to him. She loved him and sat on top of the couch right behind his head. He enjoyed me playing the piano for him and for them, and he always hummed along.

Oh, how I will miss you! I will miss your smile, your big hugs, and tender kisses on my cheeks, Rich. And your joy when you saw me walk into the living room. And as many times that I danced for them, he always cheered me on. He truly enjoyed my company. I can say that with confidence because I felt it, and I'm sure they felt my love!

My eyes are so full of tears, my face so wet, I thought about stopping to regain my composure, but I've decided to finish my meditation. Sweet Richard, you will never know the hole you left in my heart. Your seat on the living room couch will forever be empty. I'm sure your sweet Barbara is going to look for you and wonder, and wonder, and wonder some more. She loved you dearly and I know the feeling was mutual.

It is because of events like this that my job is so hard, because I don't want to lose any of them. I would keep them forever because it's hard to say goodbye to the people you love. But I know he had to go, and I know that God called him home, and I'm glad he didn't suffer long. Because five days before he passed, I had such a good time with them. I had made some videos of him and Barbara and when I left to go out of town for a few days, I gave him a hug and said, "I'll be back soon. Hold the fort down." And he laughed and said, "Don't worry. I sure will."

Well, Richard, you did not keep your promise—you didn't wait for me. YOU DID NOT WAIT FOR ME! But I know you can look down on us from heaven and see and know how much you are missed.

Goodbye, Richard. Until we meet again . . . Shalom.

THANKFULNESS

For Now, You just Need to be Fed

I'm sure if I were to ask or take a survey on how many people (and I'm referring here to women specifically), have a story to tell, the answer would be a resounding: All! We all have a story, because we all live lives on this earth full of pain and troubles. The Scripture is pretty clear, and it was Jesus who said: "In this life, you will have troubles, but take heart, I have overcome the world."

Our stories might be different, and I'm sure they are different because we all travel on our own meridian, on our own path. We have our own losses. For some, it is the loss of a marriage story. For some, it is a loss of a child story. For some, it is a financial loss story. For some, it is a poor choices story, an addiction story, idolatry stories, and so on and so forth . . .

But isn't it wonderful that God is the one writing our story? And even if we have to go down through some valleys, we read in Psalm 23: "Even though I walk through the valley of the shadow of death, He is with me . . ." Jesus is writing our story."

After having succumbed to five years of severe depression, and after the Lord pulled me out of the pit and slowly started to rebuild my life, my good friend Cora, who kept sending me messages which I ignored, reached out to me . . . again. I finally answered and she said to me, "I'm picking you up Sunday; you're coming to church with me!

My reply was, "No . . . I'm not coming. Please don't bother. I will not answer the door."

I was born stubborn. I didn't feel I was ready, because for many years I visited churches in search of a new one and I never really connected. It was not their fault, but mine. So I was not about to embark on another church-searching road. Nope, didn't have the fortitude for it. But come Sunday at ten o'clock in the morning, my phone rang. I said to her, "You said 10:15. You are fifteen minutes early. And by the way, I'm not coming."

She said, "I drove my truck here. I have the kids in the car with me. You better get yourself down here because I'm not going to church without you." Talk about another stubborn one!

We went to New Life Church in Alamo. It was so nice to see some old friends and my heart really felt peaceful in that church. At the end of the service, I saw a woman walk down the aisle whom I recognized. "Is that Cathy Estrada," I asked?

"Yep," she said.

What followed was a sweet fellowship of a reunion after about ten years or so. And what a sweet reunion it was. She invited me to go to the Dublin campus and the following Sunday I was there. I cannot tell you anything except that when I walked through those doors, I felt the Holy Spirit tell me: "Welcome home, my daughter."

Ah. I still savor that feeling. I feel it even today because there's no better emotion than to know that you belong. Cathy was right there next to me, encouraging and helping me through some very hard emotions. She said to me, "One day, I want to see you up there serving the Lord again."

And I said, "I don't think I ever want to be involved on a

stage in a worship team, to be in front of people." Been there, done that. To which she just said, "For now, you just need to be fed. For now, you just need to let God heal you. For now, just sit and take it in."

I'm sure I'm not the only one sitting in this position before the Lord. And I can tell you that He has been faithful, He has been feeding me through the messages from the pastors and through the worship music in my newfound church, through the prayers done every Sunday with faithful women like Josie, Barbara, Judy and Brenda. What a good God we serve. "He is the goodness of my life," the new Toby Mac song says, and I could not agree more.

I can and I want to encourage anyone who is going through hard times to allow God to feed you, to care for your needs wherever you are. Because He knows. Because He sees. Because He is writing our stories. I'll take comfort in knowing that He who began good work in me, will see it to completion. It is His promise.

Amen . . . Amen.

Lazy Saturdays

I had an emergency this morning—I ran out of coffee! My coffee machine malfunctioned and I had to send it back. It's a Bruvi machine—something very beautiful, but apparently beautiful does not equal sturdy. So while I was waiting for a new one to arrive, I was using my French press, and this morning I realized I was out of beans.

You know in the movies when a scene needs to be emphasized, they play this music which gets repetitively louder? Yeah, *that* music—you know what I'm talking about. I heard it in my head this morning, which constituted a trip to the coffee shop at six o'clock. I mean, my addiction cannot be interrupted. No, Ma'am, it cannot!

So, with coffee in hand and surrounded by my beautiful dogs who of course are sleeping, I am sitting at the feet of Jesus, marveling at His creation. Introspection and analysis will come a bit later, but for now, I'm just taking it all in.

My garden is the place where I hang most of the time, especially in the evening. Everything is blooming. I have four big rosebushes—one white, two pink, and one a combination of red and yellow. I wish I knew more about flowers, but I'm learning. I planted my first tomatoes this week.

I went to a junkyard in Berkeley and I bought two small wooden boxes. Yes, it is a junkyard that sells all kinds of stuff— junk—well, you know what they say: their junk, my treasures. I brought them home and had my brother Emi put wheels on them so I can move them around and five plants later, I'm sitting and enjoying the view—imagining the crops and hoping and praying for good ones. I also planted some flowers and I joyfully watch them grow every day.

I love to watch my dogs play on the lawn. I have a small water fountain and love to hear the sound of it, the sound of birds, and the sound of happy dogs. Yeah, it's come to this.

I am at least grateful I have my dogs since my family is hiding from me, all five of them. By this I mean my ex-husband, his parents, and my children.

This past week has been another emotionally taxing one. I seem to have them a lot lately. In fact, last night I was talking to myself in the mirror saying, "Why can't you get a grip and not allow situations and peoples' attitudes to affect you so negatively?" What? Nobody does this? You mean you don't talk to yourself in the mirror? Come on—please don't let me believe I'm the only one. Because I seem to just feel exhausted at the end of each week, so tired and worn out, and wanting to give up.

And coming before the Lord, singing the same melody, I know I have an audience. I know I'm not the only one. I know I have company. And no, it's not because misery loves company, it's because life is hard, is it not? I have one amazingly beautiful friend who I know struggles at the end of the week just like me! T . . . sisters for life, right?

So because it's Saturday morning and I don't have an agenda, I just sit at the feet of Jesus, coffee in hand, and let His presence wash over me. It's hard to describe it. What can I compare it to? You know how when you listen to Vivaldi's *Four Seasons*, "Winter" is melancholy. The music is mostly minor, kind of fitting the mood, but then spring comes and the notes get happy. The music builds up and in my car, when I was listening to this a few days ago, I was directing. I don't care if anyone thinks I'm crazy, I was in the moment. The music penetrated my soul and I could do nothing but be in sync with it and let my soul dance.

Yes, today it feels like Vivaldi's "Spring," because it's the end of April and spring is in the air. Yes, it is. I talk to my Lord and even though He already knows everything, He never tires, He's never bored, He's always present, He understands.

Yes, it has been a very emotionally taxing week but thank God for Saturdays. And I'm sure tomorrow, I'm gonna say thank God for Sundays, because each morning, His mercies are new. Reading Psalm 37 this morning, I tarry over these two verses:

"Delight yourself in the Lord, and He will give you the desires of your heart. Commit your ways to Him, trust in Him, and He will act." Psalm 37:4-5 ESV.

What does it mean to delight in someone? What comes to mind when you hear such a statement? Other words for it are contentment, glee, joy, satisfaction, enchantment, delectation, pleasure, and ecstasy. Wow, quite descriptive, don't you think?

Maybe I can say: I am satisfied in the Lord, I am ecstatic to be in His presence, it's a pleasure to know Him, I'm content to know He's around me, I glee with joy. Yes, today, I am all of the above. It is because of this that I can safely say, according to His promises, that He will give me the desires of my heart, He will act on my behalf, and I commit my ways to the Lord.

"Good Morning Mercy" is a song by Jason Crabb. I played it quite a bit this past week. Yes, good morning, Saturday. Though you are lazy, there are mercies bestowed on you. There is fullness of joy, flawlessness, beauty, even from ashes.

Yes,—He makes everything new. And because this is so real to me, I'm ready to start the day, energized and skipping with joy. Well, I'm actually skipping into the kitchen to make myself a new amazing latte with frothy milk. I mean, what can be better than that?

People Watching in Downtown Pleasant Hill

I have never done this. Well . . . not true . . . I have at the airports many times. But I have never taken my morning coffee (Peet's of course) and allowed myself to just sit outside and enjoy the scenery. I've always sipped mine on the go. Driving and drinking my coffee. Yeah, that is one of my favorite things to do (much to Nick's dismay in the past).

But today I've decided to just sit. Found a nice table outside the coffee shop and I was breathing it in. The air was cool. Even though it was early in the morning, for the month of June, it has been cold. Many complain when we just have 70 degrees, but for me it is perfect. The aroma of coffee satisfies my otherwise nagging angst. Yeah, this feels good . . . ahhhh.

Thank you, Lord. My job for this morning was cancelled so I had an empty calendar. Not too usual but I'm liking it. So, croissant half eaten, I watched people passing me by, many with coffees in hand looking like they are hurrying to their jobs. And then I notice their attire. So many wear their company logo I think, on their shirts.

"T-Mobile" says one on a husky man with a large bag on his shoulder who was rushing to his car. On the back, more info about the giant company. Okay, maybe he is not a T-Mobile employee but why else would someone wear such merchandise? A young man passed me by with the Boulangerie de Paris on his chest. Now this one has to work there. C'mon would you wear one like that? Nope, I would not.

Wonder how everyone feels about this one. Saw a beautiful woman wearing a white T-shirt with big bold letters saying: "Female all the way." Now this could open a deep and wide conversation about what is going on in this world today, couldn't it? Such a painful subject for me and I'm sure for a lot of people. Because to give attention to such lost souls who are claiming to "identify" or not to, to their assigned birth gender, is lunacy. It insults my intelligence and I'm sure the beliefs of many likeminded individuals.

But do I want to even attempt to debate? Do I have an audience? Does anyone even care what I have to say in the matter? Well I believe one person does and His name is Jesus Christ, the Lord. Yes, He cares to have His truth defended. Yes, He wants His children to stand against the lies so many people believe.

The enemy of our souls likes nothing more than his victims to believe lies, because he can keep them in the bondage of their own minds, in total depravity. Because we know that this "move" comes straight from the pit of hell, and we know that from the moment he was cast down from heaven, the devil never stopped undermining, stealing, and destroying God's creation. Can we all agree that he has engaged us in a war which for many was and is deceptive and worse, defeating? Yeah, I believe this to be true with all my heart.

Got distracted a bit from my people watching and as more and more people were roaming the street, I have lost interest. And I also almost finished my delicious coffee. But before I return to the tasks of the day, I will say this: I would wear a shirt that says, "For the blood of the lamb and for the saints." Because if people wear their Chipotle and Disney garb, I too can display what my heart's desires are. I do have in my closet, tops that says: Faith, The Lord is my Shepard, and Believe. And today I have made the decision to pull them out and wear them proudly. Because my Lord is worthy of being on display. Yes, He is.

Please Do Not Bring Presents
Your Presence is Enough (No Pun Intended)

Today is December 12, 2022, and I am turning fifty-six. I know my dad would have fun with the numbers because he always does. It's a passion of his, and personally I think it's so amazing. I moved into a new home last week and the plan was to celebrate my birthday on Sunday the 11th, having invited all my siblings that are local with their families, and of course, my parents.

Well, things didn't go according to plan because my mom got sick, so we postponed it until next Sunday. No problem there. Everybody agreed it was the best. The only problem was that I started feeling sick last night and today on my actual birthday, I am not feeling well. I thought about singing and recording a song here in my living room, but I am not sure my voice could handle that. I told people when preparing for Sunday to not bring any gifts because their presence would be enough. Well, I guess today I will celebrate in the presence of the Lord only.

That is quite all right. Though I miss my family, His presence is all I need at this time of need (no pun intended here) because through sickness and health, including good and bad, through ups and downs, He is faithful, He never leaves, and He is not scared of a cold. Because He is God Almighty, and I am okay right now to just be in His presence. His love comforts me and His grace and mercy sustains me. And I can tell you with firm assurance: His presence is all I need .

I am singing without piano accompaniment with a raspy voice, but in adoration, "What a good God you've been to me." Thank you, my family, for all that you have done for me, especially in the past five years. Here's to a new life—new beginnings, together with Him. I love you.

Cold Weather Equals Happiness

I don't know why, but as the season changes and winter sets in, I am being reminded of so many experiences in my life that happened during winter. My birthday is in December. My favorite season is fall-winter because here in California, fall and winter have kind of the same weather—cool, cold, yet sunny, occasionally going down to zero and below. Sadly, we don't have snow where I live, but I grew up with the rain and snow and most of my memories were fun-filled.

I remember as a child, we would always go outside and play in the snow and ice skate on the icy snowy roads with some more than laughable handmade skates (compared to today's). Building a snowman, rosy cheeks, cold hands and feet, runny noses, and even colds that we caught as children were times when my mom would make us warm tea and snuggle us in bed after she gave us homemade cold remedies. Yes, even this had a sweet connotation for me. It might sound strange, but I felt protected under my mother's wings even though I was sick.

Today I reminisce about my life so much and joy comes to mind. We came to America in December and I got engaged to Nick in January. Both events made a such tremendous impact on my life; absolutely joyful moments. We landed in Chicago in December 1985, and even though we were very poor in the beginning, we were so joyful to be here.

After escaping from the communist regime, we were

given a new chance for freedom in this life, and we didn't take it lightly. We were very blessed and worked hard to achieve the "American Dream." Looking at all my siblings and many members of my family now, I can confidently say that God has been good to us and so has America. We have been blessed to achieve the dream so many long to have.

Meeting Nick for the first time at a New Year's Eve party at his church in Brasov—ah, the memories of that particular day will be forever etched in my mind! Such emotions! For me, it was love at first sight as they say, because I looked at him and I saw something special!

He was tall, dark, and handsome, all strong desires in my book. He was thin with long hair and a beard and living his life his own way, despite being raised by a very strict religious family. I loved his big, beautiful eyes and smile, and his sense of humor. If he was at a party, he always ended up in the middle of it and he *was* the party. He made everybody laugh and of course, he got *my* attention!

I loved him then and it has continued through many decades, of course changing from puppy love to a more mature love to a love so desperate, even despite his rejection. Yet despite his rejection in the last years, he was and will forever be the one who stole my heart on a cold January night on a sleigh ride in the snow, in my city of Sibiu.

Maybe now you get the picture of how much I treasure the cold season! I love it! And today as we approach the last few months of the year, though bittersweet, I still treasure many things. I treasure the life that my Creator God gave me. I treasure the place where He has me stay. I treasure my church and my faithful friends. I treasure the sweet fellowship of the redeemed. For me, very time I leave there, I am full to the brim and actually to overflowing.

I will treasure fall this year despite the losses, and I will find new meaning to new beginnings. I know I am reaching some women right now who, like me, have been thrown into the midst of chaos, and have experienced an array of emotions. You know what I am talking about. Yeah, you — all of you.

But I am here to tell you that spring, summer, fall, or winter, God is with us! He will never leave us or forsake us. No! His promises are yes and Amen! So, whether you are happy during the cold season or you bask in the heat, the one who makes it all worthwhile is our savior Jesus!

When I Hung on the Tree, I Called Your Name Out

From an early age I loved music, and I was born into a family that loved to sing. My grandfather was a choir director and my mother and my aunt were beautiful sopranos. In fact, my parents bought a piano way before us, the children, arrived on the scene. Their desire was to instill in us, love for the instrument. Curious that neither of them played. They just had this desire, and for one of their babies, it stuck.

They sent me to the school of music and art from an early age and the education I received there I have applied throughout my life. I cannot say I am an amazing singer nor a pianist, but I love to praise His name through song.

I was asked many times to pick a favorite, but how can I? What an impossible task. No, I cannot pick one favorite but I *can* pick a hundred. Is this good? Should I start? No, I will not, because to do so would require pages and pages of scores, chords, and lyrics.

Last night at Bible Study, Cindy said something that stuck with me. She shared what the Lord whispered to her once during devotion: "When I hung on the tree, I called your name out. I called the name of your children out. I called you by name," and the song "He Knows My Name" sprung from my lips. What a beautiful ode to an amazing savior.

The lyrics say: "He knows my name, He knows my every thought, He sees each tear that falls and hears me when I call."

When I call? Of course, He hears! But Cindy said that hanging from the cross He called out my name, He called out my name! Yes, he called out our names! Yes, Christ, the son of God, hanging between heaven and earth on the cross of Calvary before surrendering His spirit to the father, amid pain and suffering, and most likely amid shadow breaths, He called out:

"Damaris, my love for you is eternal. I give up my life so you can live here on earth, but then eternally, with me, as well."

"Cindy, I have called you out of this world so you can find meaning in doing my work. Because this world with all it offers does not satisfy. No money, no shopping, no jewels, nothing and no one will give you what your soul hungers for."

"Terry, I have called and equipped you to serve your husband, but ultimately me."

"I have called your name Kim, Barbara, Marleen, Carmel, Cindy, Sal, Cathy, Dori, Ligia."

Will you answer? Will we answer? Will we fulfil our calling? And resounding through the ages the people whose names He called responded with an empathic: Yes! Here I am Lord! Use me! Mold me! Hold me! Send me! Here we are Lord! Hineni!

Even in the Valley,
He is with Me, and I will Fear No Evil

Because this long and painful journey is ending, evil intensifies. The enemy knows that he's lost his grip on me—on my mind, heart, and soul—because he came to destroy and he thought he won! But . . . God. But . . . God. What the enemy meant for evil, God, is turning into good. What Nick wanted to destroy, we got to build new.

In Isaiah chapter 61-3, we read that God will raise beauty out of ashes. Yes, He does! And I am a living testimony! I can and I will always testify about the goodness of God! I will always sing. I will always worship Him, because He and only He is worthy.

Yesterday was December 4, 2022. I have moved most of my stuff from my marital home into the rental, much to Nicks displeasure, and of course my son's. The moving company arrived around 9:30 a.m. and the whole previous night from midnight to five in the morning, Nick wanted to talk to me. I did not want to sit in the same room with him, but he insisted because we truly have not talked for many months.

Our *talk* was not a normal talk. Not what anybody would consider a normal conversation. No, because we trigger each other. Because the hatred in his heart was so deep, for five hours he just vomited anger! I cannot say that I did not react to his accusations, which I have heard over and repeatedly. I did try to reason with him, reasonably (no pun intended). I did yell and scream, telling him repeatedly that all I want is my freedom. That I want out! That this house is toxic That I cannot and will not stay here anymore.

I told him that I am moving out, partially because I do not trust him. He was very angry about things that I already took out of the house, like some of my pictures, some art, some dishes, glasses, coffee cups, and of course one of my pianos, my beautiful upright Yamaha which I relocated to my parent's house. He was mad. He was beyond mad. He destroyed things in the house because of it—yelling and screaming—because I did not ask his permission, and I did not *communicate*!

So, that morning when the moving people came, he was ready with the phone set on record, sitting behind the glass door in the kitchen and constantly yelling, "Thief!"

We made it out of the house okay, and then we unloaded at the new rental. And I saw myself pictured in this image: from my house on the hill in beautiful Lafayette, to the house in the valley in a new town, unfamiliar to me.

Lord, the Psalms are full of laments and cries for You to walk with King David, on the mountain tops but also in the valleys.

Almost picture perfect to the circumstances of my life, today.

So, again in an attitude of total surrender I cry out to Him and say:

As you were faithful to your servant of the old, so you will be to me, oh God of my salvation!

As you walked with him, many times in his valleys, you will walk with me. You will be my strength, my portion, my rock, my refuge.

In You I trust and patiently wait to see how things will unfold.

I love you, Lord! I truly do love you deeply!

He Never Let Me Down

Driving to my parents' house this morning, I hear a song on the radio with the chorus repeating this line over and over again: "You never let me down," or, "He never let me down." And the questions that popped in my head were: Did he? Does he? Will He? It might sound like a rhetorical question but is it? Because the entire human race has asked millions of times: Where are you God? Why did you let me down? Why did you not send the answer I was praying and hoping for?

Has anybody ever felt let down? Can I be honest? I *did* feel let down many times. My feelings, though genuine, beg the question, "Was it right for me to feel this way? For a Child of God to feel this way toward her Heavenly Father?" Because feelings are tricky as we all know, and to live life based solely on feelings is a disaster in waiting. Feelings. Oh, the feelings that govern our lives and take us from the pinnacle of happiness to the dumpster of pain and sadness.

But back to the question above. When a child of God feels this way, I believe it is because of a misalignment between her or him and the creator God. We are told in Psalm 139 that we have been wonderfully and fearfully made. All the days of our lives are written in His book. God knows the beginning and the end. Because He is also the Alpha and Omega.

Scriptures also tell us that you and I will encounter tribulations: pain, loss, anxiety, rejection, depression, and the list can go on and on. But, God is in total control. I believe disappointment comes when we don't get our way or when we don't get our prayers answered the way we think they should—when we have the audacity to ask the potter why did He make us this way? Me this way? Why are you molding me this way?

Sometimes I don't want to be a vase but rather a beautiful statue that sits in a beautiful, amazing garden. How about that? Anybody with me? Kind of reminds me of the Bible verse that makes a reference to the hand. Can it tell the foot what to do? Or why are you a foot and I the hand? Or even better the head? I mean without it, we would be . . . headless.

Years ago, I wrote a poem called "Disappointment." At the time, I was in a very dark valley and my writings showed that. After all, if someone sings the blues, one doesn't think it's from a point of happiness and joy. The same goes for writing. Here it is:

Disappointment has taken residence within me,
And is making herself quite at home.
I have told her to leave, to go somewhere else.
I don't like what she did to my soul.

Like a wound that is trying to close, but it can't.
Too much pressure inside, it dehisced.
It boils down in my mind and erupts every day,
With the same off-key chorus of strings.

All the tunes are the same, just the key might be changed.
All in minor of course, soft but sad.
Trying hard to erase any hope that I have,
Disappointment sings songs of despair.

I have covered my ears not to hear any more.

It distorts all the music in me.
What have you done with the music I had?
And what should I do with this bad harmony?

But as hard as I try not to listen, I hear,
Something different, a new kind of ring.
And it comes from within. I am shocked, is this true?
Are you there? Come on out, come and sing!

For your music is different and your message is strong.
Take my yoke, it is light, and you'll see.
Disappointment will flee, for it cannot survive,
With the God spirit in tandem harmony.

Like a weight lifted off from my soul I can feel,
Hope again that is sprouting from Him.
And together we sing such a sweet harmony.
Disappointment is gone, I am free.

So, just like the verses in my poem, when I choose not to
listen to my own thoughts, but to His, I need to honestly say,
"He never let me down. He will never let me down."

I Am His Girl!

In an attempt to calm my emotions down after a hard
day of negotiations and high emotions, my father sent me
some messages on my phone. He said to me: "Don't look
back . . . look forward . . . your husband didn't love you, but
God did. And He does! You are His girl!"
Such tender words coming from my father's heart. My

sweet father and mother. They walked with me through this long and hard road. Maybe I should say I dragged them through the mud with me. And they never left me, mud or not, hard or not, they stayed with me, because I was their girl, and I still am.

But I also have a Heavenly Father who loves me so much, who loves every human being so much that He gave His only son for us. So, I can be redeemed from the sinful nature and given a new name and a new heart.

I am a child of God. I am His girl. Oh yes, I am. And because I am His girl, He walks me through the valleys. He whispers, "Do not be afraid." He leads, He whispers, He nudges, like a tender parent. He encourages, He loves unconditionally, He forgives, He provides, He sees and understands, He carries, He protects, He admonishes, His promises are true, He cannot deny Himself, His word never returns void.

He gives freely, He delights in me, He loves to give good gifts to his children (yes, me), He's faithful, He never leaves, He never rejects or abandons, He rejoices over me, He gives me a new song, He will lead me on to glory, when my trumpet will sound, where He will welcome me with open arms.

Oh, where does the list stop? The magnificent character of out Heavenly Father—and our sweet Savior. I cannot wait to gaze upon His beautiful face. All because: I Am His Girl!

Can We Praise Him for the Closed Doors?

As we navigate through life and as we get closer to our final destination, I am sure all of us can write and share part of our journey. Scriptures tell us that life on this earth is full of troubles, and boy can we testify to that. I was listening to a TikTok posting this morning and one little phrase caught my attention. A beautiful lady was reading and she said, "Can we praise God even for closed doors?"

This question stayed with me and I let it penetrate deep into the depths of my being, where nobody has access but me and Him. And the questions started to pour out: "Can I really praise Him for no answers? Do we know what praising Him for no answers means?" Closed doors are hard to face! I understand, or I think I do.

Because even in the natural when you stand in front of a closed door, you can do a few things. You can knock and expect someone to open it. You can turn the handle and just walk in. You can stand in front of the door and knock and knock and wait and wait. Or you can turn and walk away, occasionally, making a decision never to return!

I'm sure there are many other options one has in front of a closed door, but these are just a few that came to my mind this morning as I was sipping my coffee, surrounded by my beautiful baby girls.

I heard the rain this morning and it's unbelievable that in California at the beginning of May, heaven decided to bless us with beautiful and amazing rain. All my plants look invigorated. I'm sure my tomatoes are dancing with joy. My flowers look just a little better—brighter, having been blessed by the heavenly water. But back to my introspection.

Closed doors! Doors that will not open again! By walking away from a closed door, we walk away from what is behind it. Pretty simple, right? Well, not if you consider this: What is behind a closed door? I'm sure there are thousands of answers and different scenarios.

Let's start to enumerate: Unbelievable joy, but also much pain. Memories, life, families, pictures frozen in time, jobs, friends, the loss of friends, old friends, beloved pets, marriages, tears and laughter, rivers of tears, disappointments, success, health or sickness, rides of joy, amazing birth moments of your children, birthdays, anniversaries, loss of children, loss of parents, loss of husbands or wives. The list goes on and on. Please add your own experiences to the list because so much more can live behind those closed doors.

"Closed doors are God's ways to eliminate options" our pastor said, and I am beginning to agree. And I'm sure for many of us, to leave closed doors behind and walk in uncertainty is extremely hard—because of the unknown! How many times have we struggled to walk away because what was behind was familiar, and even though many times it brought us down to such pits of despair, it was home? Many of us refuse to walk away from a closed door because we think that without it, we cease to exist, or have meaning!

Yet the question was asked this morning: Can we praise God for closed doors? Do we know Him deep enough to leave behind the closed door and follow Him? Do we trust when He says: "Come to me and I will give you rest for your weary souls so all the stuff behind the closed door will lose its power on us?"

Can we? Do we? Are we going to praise Him? Are we going to say, "Though I don't understand, I will praise you, Lord! Though I still want to go in, I will walk away, holding your hand, *knowing* that what You have for me is good!

The scripture says that what God has prepared for us is far better than we have ever thought or imagined! 1 Corinthians 2:9. Do we trust that? Do we even know that? Are we ready to fully surrender in front of a closed door and with a humble heart say, "Though You slay me, I will trust you!" Job 13:15. "Though I don't like it, I will praise you? I will praise you! I will praise you! Yes I will praise you!" And with the confidence that only the Holy Spirit gives, we walk away!

But before I go grab my second cup of coffee and start on my daily routine, this image of a closed door of the heart persists in my mind. The Bible says: "Behold I stand at the door and knock. If anyone hears my voice and opens the door, I will come into him and eat with him, and he with me." Revelation 3:20.

Now that is a closed door worth opening that Jesus beckons all to open. For God so loved the world that He gave His only begotten son, for whosoever believes in Him (and opens the door) shall not perish, but have everlasting life.

"Is My Love Not Enough for You, My Daughter?" asks the Heavenly Father

When God the Father, God the Son, and God the Holy Spirit were hovering over the darkness in the beginning, before all creation came into existence, they had us in mind. The Scriptures say that we were created in their image. God, the Father said: "Let us make man into our own image . . ." see Genesis 1:26-28.

I've wondered many times why God created the human race since He is, in His Trinity, self-sufficient, omnipotent, omnipresent and sovereign. Why bother with the human race, knowing that they will not be honoring and loving their Creator back?

As a mother, having been estranged from my children

for a while now, I know what it feels like to have those that I have created and raised, turn their backs on me, ignoring my existence and dishonoring me totally. Is this how God feels today? Is this how God felt through the ages?

To create something in your own image who denies your existence, is horrific and hard. I have lived and experienced this, and I know many who have had similar experiences. Yet, all of us have done it at some point in our lives. If we didn't necessarily deny Him, we definitely did not give Him the proper place in our hearts and in our lives.

As I had to sort through the feelings of rejection during the last years of my marriage, the thought of losing what I had and what I worked so hard to achieve, paralyzed me. Even though my husband was living a double life, with everyone's knowledge mind you, including mine, I did not want to be divorced. So I fought for many years to not get here.

Sadly, it was all in vain. And what I didn't realize while I was smack in the middle of it was, that my husband and my marriage became my idol—my identity, my fight, my goal, my desire, my everything. All the while pushing God on the back burner, even though I knew that doing that might cost me a lot of pain and suffering.

I thought I was doing the right thing. I mean, I was told a million times that God hates divorce, and fighting for a marriage that was decimating in our faces was, is, a godly thing to do. Right? I was praying God's will, right?

Looking back today, after I have had some time to reflect, I hear the voice of my God calling to me: "Is my love for you, my daughter, not sufficient enough? Why do you desire so desperately the love of a man, instead? Why are you pining for a man who does not pine for you? Why do you chase after something that does not satisfy? Come to me and I will give you rest.

Come to me and I will satisfy you, as with the richest of food."

And the voice of our Creator resounds through the ages for all mankind to hear. After all, He created us, and we, His creation, had chosen to ignore Him—to make Him secondary, to think that we know best and to run after our earthly desires and pleasures, believing the lie that the enemy had whispered from the beginning of creation until now:

"Surely, He did not say . . . surely, if He loved you, He would not have allowed you to go through this."

Yet, our father calls out: "Before I made you, I knew you. I have woven you and I have formed you in your mother's womb. I love you with an everlasting love, and nothing can separate me from you. No death, no famine, no sickness or wellness, no divorce, no loss of health or a job, no loss of earthly relationships, no trouble, and no money or lack thereof can separate us from the love of God who is in Christ Jesus himself." Oh, what a beautiful remembrance of his promises. See Romans 8.

So, with my heart tendered by the truth of the gospel, which says that God so loved the world (Damaris, Caleb, Adrianne, Aurel, Maria, Ligia, Ben, Mike, Chris and, Dana, Emi and David), remember that God so loved the world that He gave His only Son—the second person of the Trinity— for whosoever believes in Him shall not perish, but have everlasting life. And with the help of the Holy Spirit, the third person of the Trinity, we can live victorious lives which honor our Creator.

Yes, I love the Lord my God with all my heart and mind and soul. Not because of me, but because He loved me first. Such a great love, agape love, can only be understood when we immerse ourselves in Him.

To God Be the Glory. Forever and Ever. Amen.

Citizens of Heaven

When we left communist Romania, I remember I went with my father to pick up our passports. They were all brown and right on the covers of each was printed: "Passport for a Person without Citizenship." I guess it was a way for them to punish us because we were leaving our country, next to being considered traitors, so they made us pay to give up our citizenship voluntarily. Such a farce. I have never heard such craziness in my life. Give up voluntarily? No, it was not voluntary, but forced. Another way for the communists to punish people.

So, walking out, holding those passports in our hands, my heart full of fear, I asked my father, "Well, since we are not citizens of Romania, and neither are we citizens of America, who do we belong to? Who really cares about us in case something happens to us?" Such concerns and such hardcore questions coming from the young teenager that I was. But I will never forget my father's answer.

"It doesn't matter my daughter that they took away our citizenship. We are all by birth, Romanians, but the most important citizenship is the heaven one. We belong to God's kingdom, and thus we are citizens of heaven."

Driving from church that morning, sitting up high on a hill, we saw a beautiful American flag flying in the wind. And for a moment, I just felt so proud to be an American citizen. Because a few years after we arrived in Chicago, America allowed us to become citizens by naturalization. What a proud moment it was, being sworn in, in San Francisco, surrounded by hundreds of people who felt honored to be now called Americans.

Despite anything that is going on, I still love this country because I consider it as my own. America has been good to us, and it has embraced us with open arms. The land of opportunity indeed for all who want to come here and work hard to achieve the American dream. It is possible, it is achievable, by the grace of God, but also by consistent, diligent hard work and discipline.

I am proud to be an American today, and I pray blessings over this country. I pray for the people in government, I pray for the people in positions of leadership. I pray that my religious freedom will continue to be allowed to manifest, because this is one of the reasons why my father, surrounded by his wife, eight children, and speaking no language, took us from the heart of Transylvania to the land of the free, my America the beautiful.

And to my friends who take everything we have for granted, simply because they do not know the difference, I am here to tell you that we are blessed, and America is still the greatest country in the world, and the best place to worship and raise your family.

Here's to many more years to come!

The Journey to Forgiveness

After leaving church this morning, I came straight home. There was a burden in my heart to write . . . I always joke that I walk into church with make-up on, and I come out sans, because all is washed out as I pour my heart out to my Lord, in prayer and worship, and today was no exception. The subject was one of my biggest struggles—forgiveness, and I am sure it is for many others as well.

One of the most quoted passages of scriptures is 1 Corinthians 13. It's being recited at weddings, sung in so many versions and memorized by many. I do remember it being one of Nick's favorites. Sadly, he was always telling me that my love (not his) should resemble 1 Corinthians 13: "Love is patient, love is kind, it does not envy, it does not boast . . . it keeps no record of wrongs . . . love does not delight in evil but rejoices with the truth . . . "

Not keeping records of wrongdoings done to us is hard, because our human tendency is to remember, and to remember it well. I don't know about you, but I have a good memory when it comes to offenses and wrongs done to me. Anybody else? And walking the dark and hard road of divorce, one can only imagine the feelings of hurt.

To not tally up the offenses is to have the heart and mind of Christ. Forgiveness is a command, and we are required to always forgive. Forgiveness is hard, but not impossible, and if Jesus commands us, He will also help us grant it, regardless of how we feel in the beginning.

Many years ago, as I received biblical counseling in my own home due to my inability to go to church because of a chronic illness, my beautiful, amazingly talented counselor had me memorize the following verse: "Get rid of all bitterness, rage, anger, harsh words, and slander, as well as all types of evil behavior. Instead, be kind to each other, tenderhearted, forgiving one another, just as God through Christ has forgiven you." Ephesians 4:31-32 NLT.

Two key words for me here: bitterness and forgiveness, and I think everybody can guess why. Because by holding on to unforgiveness, roots of bitterness grow—roots of resentment, of abandonment, of pain, and even hatred. And they all have one thing in common: Not letting us forgive the offenses done to us most of the time by the people closest to us, by the people whom we love the most. So many images go through my mind, so many stories of hurt told by a very broken, rejected, and replaced wife.

Having experienced the break of the marriage covenant, due to adultery, one's heart grows bitter fast. I grew revengeful, especially towards the person who took my place. It's really strange that I can forgive my husband, and I say this today for I have worked hard to be here, but I struggle to forgive the women that enjoyed my husband in my place.

Why? Why them and not him? And I think the answer is quite simple: Because it was him, *I loved*. And like I said, I worked at being in this space. But regardless of my feelings, we are commanded to forgive all who have sinned against us and have wronged us. Forgiveness is hard, but not impossible, and it bears rewriting and repeating.

There were many, many verses in the Scripture about the importance of forgiveness. One of the most important I believe is in the Lord's Prayer: "Forgive us our iniquities, as we also forgive those who trespass against us . . . "

Wow. So I am called to forgive as a response to being fully forgiven by Him first. I am called to forgive because of what Christ did on the cross for me. I am called to release the load and remember the price that my Lord Jesus paid for me on Calvary. He suffered and gave his life so I can live . . . free, yes free.

I love a quote by Tim Keller who said: "Forgiveness is a form of voluntary suffering." Yeah, it is. It was for Christ, and it should be for us. But we have grace that helps us, and the grace bestowed upon us will fill and help us.

But like the message this morning in church said, and I quote: "If we have clogged arteries of unforgiveness, grace cannot flow through. We are not only called to forgive, but ultimately to bless. For being blessed by His grace, we too are to bless others."

Now here is where I struggle a lot. To bless? No, Lord, I can't! To bless the woman who lived with my husband for many years, knowing full well that he was still married? This is too much!

Please don't ask me to do this because I cannot.

Yet, God doesn't change His mind and His Word is everlasting. "You have heard that it was said, 'Love your neighbor and hate your enemy.' But I tell you, love your enemies and pray for those who persecute you . . . " Matthew 5:43-48 NLT.

Jesus came to fulfill the Old Testament but some of the commandments given in the old times He enhanced to something more beautiful and much simpler. It used to be an eye for an eye and a tooth for a tooth, but Christ changed it to: "Love your enemy and pray for them. Bless them."

Maybe simpler, but not easier.

Jesus also said that those who love Me, will obey My commandments. So, if forgiveness is a command, how do I obey it? How do I fulfill it? I believe every one of us has their own journey to grant forgiveness, because we have all experienced offenses in many different ways. But the commandment is for all, regardless of our pain and suffering. Regardless, no matter what.

Wake up my soul today and choose to forgive. Walk the journey of forgiveness in the company of Him who loves to journey with you. So, kneeling at the altar today, I prayed blessings over those who have done wrong to me, and from the bottom of my heart, I say: "I forgive you, N, M, CJ, GP and J. I forgive all women who basked in my husband's love. Today I choose to forgive. Yes, Lord, I obey.

And the song that I've been singing lately rings in my heart and brings such joy. So bowing in worship I sing:

Grace, grace, God's grace

Grace that will pardon and cleanse within

Grace, grace, God's grace

Grace that is greater than all my sins.

And the ugly root of bitterness lays uprooted in the street.

And the Word Became Flesh and Dwelt Among Us

In a manger, in the town of Bethlehem, the cries of a new-born baby filled the air. Two young parents welcomed their firstborn into the world. But He was no ordinary newborn because the world was created by Him. He was the Word, who like John says in his first chapter was with the God, and the Word was God. It almost sounds like a play on words but if you read carefully, the first few verses of the Gospel of John all make sense. The Word was Jesus and Jesus was with God, and Jesus was God.

Having almost finished Bible study about the Trinity, this really jumps out everywhere from the pages of the Scripture. Trying to imagine the Creator in the form of a newborn baby makes for a good movie for Christmas, some beautiful songs, Christmas carols, and cards.

How many pictures have been painted through the centuries depicting baby Jesus? Surrounded by animals in swaddling clothes, some even pictured Him shivering because of His environment! Laying in hay! I don't know that any of this was true, and I don't think it's that important. More important is that the divine came down in the body of a newborn baby. Took on flesh and yes in the beginning, beautiful flesh—baby flesh.

I don't know why I'm so hung up on this, this morning. This imagery is not leaving my mind. And other than the shepherds visiting and later the Maggi, not much was given in the Bible about the life of Jesus as a baby, as a young child, if you wish, the son of God, the son of David, the son of Joseph the Son of Mary. We see them fleeing to Egypt to escape the wrath of Herod. We see Jesus in the temple at age twelve, engaging with the priests and the people there. And then, we see Him starting his public ministry when He was thirty years old. Everything else is left to our human imagination as far as his early life was concerned.

I know many wonder just like I do, what was Jesus like growing up? What was He like as a young boy? A teenager? A young adult? What did He do? How did He live His life? How did He relate to his parents? His siblings? His relatives?

Many were wondering when they saw Him perform miracles, asking, "Is He not the son of Josef the carpenter?" And if his father was a carpenter, did Jesus help him? Did the one who created the human body, take wood and fashion a beautiful piece of furniture? Carpentry deals with wood. I'm wondering what his father, earthly father that is, made out of wood.

And how did Jesus handle being a human and divine at the same time? The Bible says he was tempted just like us, but without sin. My mind goes to many places. There are so many questions I would ask the Lord if I had the chance to interview him. Did He obey his mother? Did He obey his father? How did He relate to his younger siblings? Did Jesus ever get sick? He who healed sickness and raised the dead . . . hmmmm.

I don't know about this, but we know the Bible is silent when it comes to this. No information given! Because it wasn't important? My inquiring mind wants to know. The Lord gave me a vivid memory and imagination.

It's Him. He poured it into me. I always say you cannot teach talent. And it's true. Just as true is one being anointed because it is not the work of men but of the Holy Spirit. Plain and simple and true. I know I'm speaking to someone today.

Jesus is truly the reason I'm alive today because darkness had engulfed me and the enemy of my soul wanted to destroy me. So I sing with all fervency. Nothing but the blood! Nothing but the blood! Nothing but the blood!

And today, I am content and want to be better. Not for me, but for the kingdom of God. I want to occupy until He comes back, like Amir Tsarfati always says. I borrowed the sentence from him.

Yes, I want to do KINGDOM work, like my good friend Dori says. While I wait for the divorce process to be finalized, and it looks like it is going to drag on for many more months to come. As per his wishes, I will wait, but not in vain. No, I will wait by being busy—spreading the gospel, helping the sick and the poor, blessing my church and its leaders. And also, I will plan to enjoy the ending of this year. A year of the favor of the Lord. A year of amazing favor.

Because He came down and walked the roads in Jerusalem and surrounding cities with one main purpose in mind—to save souls. And we are to follow suit. Will you join me?

Twenty-Eight Years Ago, Today!

Home

Tears flow down my face as I'm holding my dogs close to me. I scroll through pictures; they are beautiful pictures telling the story of a happy family—old pictures, but sadly, not too many recent pictures. No matter, my heart feels both joy and sadness, brokenness and hope, despair and peace—the kind only God can give, surpassing understanding, amazing shalom!

She was born at 9:30 in the morning in the operating room at Kaiser Hospital in Walnut Creek. Strapped to the table and separated by the sterile field, she was first seen by her father. He always bragged that he saw her first! Click, click, the camera rolled, along with the Canon video-cam! Click. Click.

And after they took her to get her cleaned up, I asked to see her. Wrapped in her new baby blanket she was absolutely beautiful—round face, beautiful eyes, and the most adorable lips. Simply beautiful! But then, what mother does not see her child like that?

We stopped using any means of protection for three years, and when the news came that I was pregnant, I was filled with joy. There is an indescribable bond between mother and child from the moment of conception, but more so when the mother starts feeling the baby move. Such joy! Such nervous expectation! Such exhilaration.

My pregnancy was not easy because my job was hard, and I couldn't rest.

I couldn't sleep well during the day as I was still working

the graveyard shift! We wanted to find out if we had a boy or a girl, but all the ultrasounds could not tell us because she was a breech baby, a stubborn little girl from the womb. Manual inversion did not work out and believe me they tried, but she wouldn't budge. So, onto surgery I went!

I remember picking up this most beautiful mossy green leather bag to pack her things in, a bag that still sits in my closet today. It is just as beautiful as in the beginning. Nice things cost money they say, so you pay for that, I guess. No expense was spared for her, from the Bellini baby furniture, to the stroller, to the clothes and plush toys! None! After all, she was our firstborn!

Because I had an elective C-section, I picked her birthday—February 16, 1995! I didn't want her on Valentine's Day, and I didn't want to wait for her to come too close to my due date which was on the 22nd, for fear that I would go into labor, something that was not necessary.

Back in my room that evening, still hooked up to some pumps and catheters but holding her into my arms, I marveled at her beautiful round eyes which seemed to follow me everywhere. It seemed that way to me, anyway! They were big, dark, brown, beautiful, round eyes. Then suddenly, for a moment, I was filled with panic, thinking that this little creature was totally dependent on me. I would be the one to feed her, to hold her, to change her, and everything else that comes with a new baby.

Flowers, toys, and small gifts filled my room. But the most precious gift was my beautiful Adrianne Nicole. She got her first name to honor her grandfather whose name is Adrian, and her middle name to honor her father whose name is Nicolae. Adrianne Nicole . . . Adrianne Nicole.

Today your mother misses you so much and sends you

many wishes of good health, steady and fulfilling employment, good and faithful friends, and good cheer. May your celebration be filled with joy, may the Lord bless you and keep you, and may He shine His face upon you and give you peace! Shalom!

Love,
Mom

Prune Me Fast, Lord

I want to be a gardener. My life has changed a whole lot lately and I've always desired to be able to grow beautiful plants and flowers. Never had a green thumb, though. I love flowers and I grew up with a mother who had beautiful plants all over our home—my sweet mom. Not busy enough raising and caring for eight children, she made time to nurture and keep amazing plants.

I remember one which sat on top of our armoire and wrapped around the whole room. It was some kind of ivy masterfully hung close to the crown molding in my room—so beautiful, so green, and so vibrant.

I was told plants respond well to sun, water, and music. Yes, you read it right—music. I have played piano ever since I was a little girl, and was blessed to have it in my room. In Romania, homes did not have the same kind of design we have here. We had no living room or family room, no dining room or office space. But we had other rooms, and each had their meaning and use.

Our bedroom (mine and my sister Ligia's), was where the grand piano sat. Yes, it did. A majestic, beautiful, brown wood piano. It was expected that the room would be clean at all times, because all guests were invited upstairs to our room for worship and full gatherings. Yes, my American friends, our grand piano in my country was in my bedroom—gasp—but it was very normal.

I asked my father what brand our piano was but he could not remember. What he shared with me was that the famous Romanian composer Nicolae Moldoveanu, was the one who tested the piano and said that it was good. Oh, and it *was* good—truly, it was an amazing piano.

But back to my plants. In the "Book of Genesis," the Bible tells us that God created the plants, the trees, and all vegetation on earth, on the third day. God also created a garden where He placed His first creation, called the Garden of Eden. For thousands of years, people tried to imagine the beauty of this place. Makes for good movies and books, with each writer painting luscious, amazing images of this world landscape.

Agh . . . how many of us still long for that amazingness? But after the fall, creation changed. The curse was placed on the first man and woman and on everything that surrounded them. That meant that humans and vegetation died spiritually, and of course physically. How aware are we today of that? Are we aware and affected by how fleeting life is? How short? Here today. . . gone tomorrow. Like grass, the Bible says, that withers like a flower that fades.1 Peter 1:24. Like a vapor which appears for a little while, then vanishes away. James 4:14.

When Jesus lived on this earth, two thousand years ago, he made the following statement:

"I am the true vine keeper, and my Father is the gardener. We tend to our vines, so they can produce much fruit."

I don't know much about wineries, but I have seen the vines being cut and cleaned so the following season they will produce more grapes. I don't know too much about roses either, but I know that any rosebush that looks amazing has been cut down and pruned so it would give the beautiful, fragrant, colorful flowers. Applied to us and in the words of Jesus, we too are being cleaned, cut down, dug around our roots, mulched, uprooted and replanted, fed and tended to.

Jesus also said that the Father disciplines those whom He loves. May be hard to swallow, but so applicable to our natural lives. Can I get an amen? I know many parents agree. I also know many parents, myself included, did not apply this biblical principle as it was intended to be.

So, what does pruning a vine or a rosebush or any plant look like? And how does the pruning of a child of God look like? I'm pretty sure it's different for all of us. Many similarities, yet different. Because we are all made in the image of our Creator, but we are nothing alike. Our fingerprints are different, our looks are different, our blueprints are different. We are all made of the same material, yet amazingly, distinguishably different, because pruning for me looks different than for you. The master gardener *has to*, and I repeat, has to, cut many times where it hurts to produce the image that best reflects Him.

In a poem I wrote years ago I said:

"He said, if I stay in his word, if I listen,
His Holiness will reflect upon me,
Like a mirror reflects the image of a vessel,
Standing face-to-face with it perfectly."

You got the image, right?
I hope you do.
I know I do.
Because I do . . .
I know that what He, my marvelous Creator does, is necessary.
(Sorry for the play on words.)

"Let's cut here to excise her desire to self-condemn," the Father says to the Holy Spirit. "Let's cut here to remove the self-imposed regrets of a painful past, most of which was out of her control."

The Holy Spirit nods. "Yes, indeed, it was."

"How about this one? How about this branch of the de-sire to control, to know, her curiosity that so many times got her in trouble? Let's prune this one for sure. Oh, and while you are there, cut the thorn of the militant spirit gone awry because that spirit is good when well-controlled by the Holy Spirit."

"That's good, that's good," they all agree in tandem.

And with gentle hands that only a gardener has for his flowers, they perform the necessary yet painful and hard process of beautifying the creation gone wrong since the fall in the garden—masterfully, with precision, right on, not making one mistake. Skilled with hands that need no guid-ance because they know the blueprint. I was created won-derfully in my mother's womb, knitted together by my Creator's love for His creation . . . perfect.

Ahhhhh . . . to be restored to a perfect relationship with Him is my deep heart's desire. And I'm sure it is the same for many of my family and friends, brothers and sisters in Christ. And I say for all, who one day want to behold His glory.

With the blood of Jesus sprinkled on the mercy seat and the eyes of my heart illuminated by the love of Christ, I surrender to the process, as long as it takes, as painful as it is, almost not hearing the cry from far away: Do it fast Lord, do it fast. Because when you prune us, you do it with such comfort and gentleness. You are a sweet, sweet, Father, gardener, grower of seeds, restorer of roots, bulbs, trees, plants, and flowers with a myriad of colors.

And because You love us, you pluck us out, and realigned us. He wants us to be fully alive.

So, prune away Lord at our lives because we know that in the end, we will reflect Him.

And He is worth, hurting for.

Breaking the Alabaster Jar

Ever since I can remember, the story of the alabaster jar from the gospels appealed to me. I have a vivid imagination; I've always had it. I pictured her, a beautiful woman with long, luscious hair. Dark. Strong.

I always thought that alabaster was the color blue. I don't know why, I just did. Back in my childhood, we didn't have google and even as I matured, I never bothered to check. Alabaster . . . blue. That's that. It made for some beautiful pictures in my mind.

I've construed that her vase was a deep blue. Small, but crafted so it fit in her gentle hands. The gospels do not name her, but it is assumed she was Mary. In fact, the Gospel of Luke calls her a very sinful woman. And when she heard that Jesus was in the house of Simon the Leper, she entered and prostrated at His feet. The author said she washed His feet with her tears, wiped them with her hair, and poured the nard over them.

The gospel of Matthew tells us that she poured it over his head. I believe she anointed his head and feet and in the words of Jesus and she prepared his body for burial. They were about to enter Passover and it was the week before His crucifixion.

I can sense the beautiful smell of the nard. I imagine all those men reclining with Jesus at the table, being pleasantly surprised by the beautiful aroma in the room. But one disciple said, "This expensive oil could have been sold and money given to the poor, Judas," and right after this incident, he betrayed Jesus. And he was the one responsible for the money—in charge of the bag. Judas—his heart, though in the presence of the divine for three years, remained dark, and un-surrendered.

"Go in peace," the Lord told the woman. "Your sins are forgiven!" Go in peace Mary, Damaris, Cathy, Cora. Go in peace, Crina, Josie, Dori, Brenda, Barb, Ligia, Laura, Naomi, Esther, and Shawana. Your sins, though many, have been washed clean by my bloodshed on the Cross of Calvary. Go in peace. Your faith has saved you. Entering His presence in an act of total surrender, my heart is filled with His mercy and overpowered by His grace, passing the gates of praise into His sanctuary, I pour the alabaster jar of my heart at the feet of my resurrected Christ.

I am in owe of His beauty. Beholding His glory, I say, "You are awesome in this place, Mighty God. You are awesome in this place, Abba Father, You are worthy of all praise. To you our lives we raise. You are awesome in this place, Mighty God!

Holy Spirit, I have been set free! Hallelujah! Hell lost

another one! Hallelujah! Hineni! Here I am Lord! The shekinah glory of your presence fills the heaven and the earth. Glory, Glory, Glory. Sing . . . shout. Sing . . . shout. Glory Hallelujah. We worship with the elders and the heavenly hosts. You are worthy, worthy, worthy. Thank you, Jesus, that you put me back together better than before. You have made me beautiful. In your eyes, Lord, I am. He did not see any worth in me, but *You* did and do!

Glory. Hallelujah. You are my redeemer! You came close to a leper like me and made my flesh new! Made beauty out of ashes! I present my body as a living sacrifice! Holy Spirit rest on me, rest on me, rest on me. Fill me to overflowing. And the aroma of my praise filled the temple. He inhabits the praises of His people. Glory! Hallelujah!

My alabaster jar, which I have come to understand is the color of a natural cream stone, broke on the altar! In total oneness with Him, I lingered in His presence! I never wanted to leave. The smell of heaven permeated my whole being. I'm not sure how long it passed. But after what seemed to be an eternity and also just a minute, I walked away . . . whole!

Crossing Over Into 2023

One of the things people do at the end of any year is reminiscing. They generally go back to the beginning of that year and try to just summarize, put into perspective, analyze, draw conclusions, and with their minds and hearts, draw a line and say, "This was a good year!" Or they might say, "This was a hard one," or they might even say, "Compared to other years, this was not too bad or maybe it was much worse."

I will go back to the end of last year when for the first time I crossed into 2022, alone, at home, and did not feel that horribly lonely. It was the first time I was home alone, and I was not wallowing in pain or letting my mind go to wondering about where Nick was and what he was doing. No, for the first time crossing into 2022, I had the confidence that this year would be different. And different it was!

One might ask, "In a good way?" Well, the word of God says in Romans 8:28 that all things work together for good. So then if I apply and believe what the Bible says, this year was a good year because this year God called me out of the grave, and when I heard his voice saying, "Damaris come forth," I came out running!!! Yes, I did!

I like my brother Ben's analogy: "You came out for fresh air after a very long time. Like Jonah from the belly of the fish, you were spewed on the shore of life where you took amazing deep breaths of fresh air."

What a true analogy! Thank you, Ben! I can tell you that it felt good to breathe clean air, to feel alive, and to know that He who pulled me out of the mire will not leave me nor forsake me but will lead me! What a glorious promise! He led me out of that pit into freedom—freedom of my mind, freedom of my soul, freedom from my burdens, freedom to follow Him, freedom from fear and anxiety, freedom from depression, freedom from oppression, freedom from abuse.

Freedom. Such a sweet word! The Bible also says that we will know the truth and the truth shall set us free. Yes, indeed! Because my freedom only came after I totally surrendered and accepted the will of God for my life, even if it did not match or fit my own.

Looking back today, as we crossed into 2023, I live in a new home—a beautiful home that I received (rent) as a result of much prayer and because God delights to give good things to His children! I rented this beautiful home and moved in at the beginning of December.

Oh yeah, did I forget to mention that I was freed from the fear of living alone? All the years that Nick was unfaithful, even though I hoped and prayed for a reconciliation, I always dreaded that *if* things didn't come through, I might have to live alone. But glory hallelujah, the Lord has freed me from that!

Today as I hear the fireworks outside, and as I lay in bed, then sitting up, having just finished my nebulizer treatment, with the floor of my room covered in tissue, still coughing and wheezing, I don't even have to look up to heaven because I know that Jesus is here with me. The Holy Spirit lives in me, and I can confidently say, "I am not alone!

Kari Jobe's song rings in my ears: "I am not alone . . . you will go before me, you will never leave me," because you, my Lord, my Savior, my God and Holy Spirit, are here with me! And what better company than to be in the presence of the Triune, Three In One, Father, Son, and Holy Ghost!

As I lay me down to sleep, I whisper, "Thank you, Lord. Thank you, Lord. Thank you, Lord. May Your will be done in my life, in the year we just entered! May You be glorified in everything that I am and do. Because You are worthy! Eben Ezer! Soli Deo Gloria!

I Am Thankful

Today as I sit and meditate, I can pen down these thoughts, these emotions. I'm thankful for being the daughter of the King of Kings and Lord of Lords. I'm thankful that

I'm saved, not because I deserve it, but because He loved me first! I'm thankful that He called me out of prison, the prison of my mind and soul, and that He continues to change me every single day. I'm thankful to be alive. I'm thankful I get to experience life next to such amazing people. I'm thankful for my parents, of course, and for my brothers and sisters.

I am thankful for Dori, my mentor, my friend, my prayer warrior. I would not understand the word of God the same without your wisdom. You are a breath of fresh holiness. You have taught me so much and I don't know how I can ever repay you. I'm thankful for Shy. She has been used by God in amazing ways to help me see, experience, and walk out into the light of freedom. Shy, you rock! I'm thankful for Laura. She is an old/new friend. We have so many things in common and I look forward to a deeper and stronger relationship. Because after all, she is my church buddy.

I am thankful for Lori, from Boston and her sweet mother Lucy. Her accent is so dear to me. I told her I would love to experience Massachusetts with her. Nothing better than having a local show you the beauty of that place. I am so glad she is in my life. Forming my single girls club.

I'm thankful to be in this position even though it's hard. I'm thankful for the house I have rented. I'm thankful for being able to move into it. I'm thankful for getting my home ready to be sold. I'm thankful for a big chapter of my life closing and a new one opening. New life is the name of my church, and it represents what I'm experiencing right now. New Life. Yes, indeed.

I'm thankful for being able to play the piano and sing again, because I was mute for many, many, years, due to my pain. I am thankful for my students, who allow me to be part of their journey to excellence. Their love for the piano and music, excites me. I look forward to tomorrow. I want to celebrate my life with you. I look forward to your visits into my new home. Life is hard at many times for many of us, but God is so, so good! Yes, He is!

Glory to His name!

THE UGLINESS
OF THE "D" WORD

I Speak English, You Speak Chinese

The story tonight has a different twist. It's called: "I speak English, You Speak Chinese." Even though I was discharged from the hospital with clear orders to rest and not make any efforts to stimulate and increase my symptoms, I had to go and "be" at the business for a few hours.

The text simply asked me: "What plans you do have to be here, so I can take care of the pressing issues that need to be solved today?"

"I will come," I said.

"Please let me know what time."

"Two-thirty, but I will not do any work as I am supposed to rest," I answered.

It's okay. You don't need to," was the reply.

How foolish I was to believe that, because the minute I walked in, the needs were visible, and everyone was so happy to see me.

"I'm here," I said. "How is everyone doing?"

Everyone answered that they were fine, except the sweet little woman whose neurons don't connect well. She was very agitated, so I decided to invite the rest to go out to the garden.

"Let's go," said two of the ladies, sounding excited, but the gentleman declined.

To say that we had a blast outside would be an understatement. Drinking Coke and eating cookies, we shared stories and laughter. Then someone called out to me and said, "You are needed inside." And what started then, was a few hours of helping, lifting, beautifying, assisting, visiting with families, talking with them on zoom, and yes, playing the piano.

One would ask: Was there a problem? If I was not sick, if all was well, no, but I was still sick. Waves of anger engulfed me. "Lord, you said to rest. But like this? I don't want to be mad, but . . . " They returned while I was still working, and the caregivers asked me if anything was needed.

"You can get dinner started," I said.

What followed in the next few minutes startled me to say the least. One of the helpers very angrily said, "I can't do this! I won't do this! I can't lift her ten times a day," referring to the new client.

What are you talking about? The look on her face showed everything. Frustration! Lord, where is this coming from? I didn't ask her to do anything. The new lady, with supervision, walks by herself. Slowly, but she does. She was very inappropriate, and I had to stop her. Not here, not now. Family is visiting. Please stop!

Later, in the front quarter, I was very short of breath. It was then that I realized that he had left. Augh! Lord? I can't do this! I called him to ask if he emailed the papers that were so important to be sent, but there was no answer. So I sent a text saying: "Need to talk, please respond!" He needed to be here for the discussion with the caregivers.

What follows is hard to describe. He walked in mad. "What is the problem?" he asked. "Please, we need to talk in your parent's room. It's the only private place in the house."

I know I had decided not to engage with Nick—to be silent—but when my own health was at stake, when I was being totally taken advantage of, I had to draw the line. No! I won't accept this as normal, and when they started to gang up against me, I lost it.

There is no need to go into any details, especially about how he and his father were on the same page—to accuse, to mar, to bring to the surface the ugliness of past sins. I cried, "I can't win this. It's three against one!"

"I agree with you," a fearful voice came.

Shocker! Nick's mom was on my side. "The caregiver is rude," she said. Okay. At least here I have some support. Even typing this at this moment, my heart skips beats because Dana, I saw in his eyes, pure hatred, and the definition of evil. My whole body, mind, and soul shook!

"It is finished," Christ said, hanging between heaven and earth, giving up his body for the love of humanity.

I too have decided the same, but for a different reason. It was for the love of myself (yes, I said it, for the love of myself), because to love others as Christ instructed us, we have to first love ourselves.

Am I making sense to you? Please write in your response, because there is no need to stick around if by this time everyone speaks Chinese and I speak English. Or was it the other way around? It really does not matter anymore. Please pray with me for wisdom and for the right people to come around.

I love you, Sis! With God on my side and support from my friends and family, we will be more than conquerors. By the blood of the Lamb and by the power of their testimony, the enemy was defeated. Hallelujah! Revelation 12:11.

Today I wanted to give up.

I find myself getting more and more angry in the last few weeks.

As much as I try to control these feelings, they are relentlessly beating me up!

The all too familiar voices which start just as a small thought, a whisper, grow aggravatingly louder:

"You should not have to do this... not now... you can't really take this burden on... I mean... c'mon.... you need peace and since she came, your life has been turned upside down!!!

Tell her she is too much ... call people and tell them you can't do this... they will understand, don't you think?"

Will they?

And ultimately what is it that I want them to understand?

Let's see:

For months I prayed with deep groanings for my children.

At home, at church, on the prayer lines on the phone, in the car ... all the time everywhere!

I prayed for their eyes to be opened to see.

I mean we sing the amazing grace song at so many occasions invoking:

"I once was lost but now I'm found.

Was blind but now I see..."

Part of my testimony is that He opened my eyes to my idolatry, and I finally surrendered though, it took me many long and painful years.

And today sitting across from me on the living room couch, was a "blind" young woman!

And I was frustrated and angry!

I can almost hear the Holy Spirit (wait a minute... I did hear Him) say:

Remember when you were there?

Have you forgotten where He brought you up from?

And most importantly you do know that you are here for a reason and God has a plan.

Live what you preach my daughter, I've heard the Lord say.

Live what you preach!

I told her to repeat the above lines for her own life and today I was to deny that they too, apply to my life?

Pretty hypocritical don't you think?

Oh, the voices of old.

The accusatory voices I knew all too well.

Almost to not give them a foot in the door I retorted:

"There is therefore no condemnation now for those who are in Christ Jesus..." wrote apostle Paul.

It is written replied Jesus ... and he had to leave ...

It is also written I replied,

"Though, I fall I will get up."

And,

"I can do all things through Christ who gives me strength"

And as with a shriek and with their heads bowed, they left me alone!

Augh the sweet fragrance of the Word permeated the house.

The alive, powerful Word of God!

It will not return void and it will never change!

It's immutable.

Everlasting.

The beginning and the end.

The Alpha and Omega.

The house is quiet now and all are asleep.

From the baby birds on the door, to the sweet doggies and to the beautiful long haired amazingly loved, young woman sleeping on the soft white sheets in an equally beautiful room.

All is quiet!

Just how I like it!

I take my time to sit at His feet and talk to Him.

And in this posturing all fears are gone...

And , all anger subsided...

I Want to Run

I want to run away from the pain. I want to run away from reality. I want to run away from the nagging feeling telling me that I am not the same. I want to run from the truth that my husband found comfort in the arms of another. I want to run so I don't feel the heaviness of the divorce. I want to run away and hide. I want to run, and run, and run.

Many years ago, I was training to run a marathon. I raised a lot of money for the American Heart Association and I started my training. Week after week my body got stronger. Day after day I ran my allowed time and at the end, I had so much energy, I wanted to keep on running. Oh, I remember that feeling — the endorphins kicking in. Do you know that feeling? Total elation!

And then the unthinkable happened — I fell! During my

training, I fell and twisted my ankle. And stubborn as I was, I did not stop training. I ran with a swollen, wrapped ankle. And to my disappointment, I could not do my time as planned. I lagged behind, and I finally had to admit to my team that I was dropping off—but not until I ran half of the marathon, not in Hawaii as it was originally planned, but here locally.

I barely made it. But at the end, I was proud of my accomplishment. I ran! I finished! And I got a small prize. Then I went home and nursed my painful ankle for many months until it got to a state of not hurting.

In the Bible, we read about running our race to the finish line, which is at the crossing into eternity. This kind of run is not optional. And for the children of God, it is not a race we can opt out of. No matter the pain, no matter the injuries, we are admonished to run the good race of faith.

Looking ahead to the prize, Apostle Paul said in 2 Timothy 4:7-8: "I have fought the good fight, I have finished the race. I have kept the faith. Now there is in store for me the crown of righteousness which the Lord will award to me on that day."

I want to run that race. I am running that race, the race that leads and gives the eternal prize. And it was still him who said in 1 Corinthians 9:24-27: "Do you now know that in a race all the runners run, but only one gets the prize? Run in such a way as to get the prize. Everyone who competes in games goes to strict training. They do it to get a crown that will not last, but we do it not to get the crown that lasts forever. Therefore we do not, unlike someone who runs aimlessly, do not fight like a boxer beating the air . . ."

So this begs the question: How are we supposed to run? Many books have been written and the fitness industry is booming with billions of followers. But are we called to train like them? Like the runners? Both my children are personal trainers. I did, in the past, train with my son, and he was merciless.

"Come on, Mom, you can do this." he would say.

"Just give me longer rests " I would ask.

"No, no time to rest too much, and in thirty seconds to one minute, we will do it again," he would reply. And I have to say that this kind of training, paired with a healthy diet, yielded results.

But we are also called to train our *souls*, to train so we can accomplish the work which was started and will be finished in us. But for this to happen, we need to be connected to our personal trainer, the Holy Spirit.

Yes, He is called our Comforter, but He is also our teacher. He guides us in truth and knowledge. He is the source of wisdom, power, and revelation. He dwells in us. He helps with our weaknesses and intercedes for us. And He also sanctifies and enables good fruit in our lives.

I want to be the trainee of Him. And I can say with confidence today that I am in the race for the ultimate prize. And for this I run! Glory to Him who is able to give me strength and who will run alongside me to eternity.

The God Who Sees—Jehovah El Roy

I often wondered about the story of Hagar from the Old Testament and marveled at how God reached down to a servant girl. Brought over from Egypt to be a slave to Abraham's wife Sarai, she was borrowed to give an heir to her childless mistress. With the mindset of a twenty-first century woman, it's almost impossible to imagine and accept such a thing. Life in the era before Christ was so different and so very hard for some—very hard.

Her name was Hagar. The Bible describes Sarai as a very beautiful woman, but does not mention if Hagar was pretty. A purchase—that's how she is described, bought as a slave. In ancient times, to be barren was almost looked upon as a curse. Sarai was barren, so she had this grandiose idea to have her husband give her an heir using her maidservant. The Bible says that he went in to be with Hagar and she conceived. Wow. Can you imagine being in her shoes?

Her master's husband slept with her, and she found herself pregnant. That was her master's wish. She had no rights, no opinion, no choice. I imagine she could not say, "No, I do not want this. Thank you, but no."

I cannot imagine being in her shoes, but I can understand that after she found herself pregnant, she looked with contempt upon her mistress. Because she finally had something Sarai did not—a baby in the making. And our beautiful Sarai dealt harshly with Hagar, and she fled.

Running away from problems is never a good idea I myself found out, because the problems come with you, do they not? Do I hear an amen? So pregnant and desolate, she found herself in the wilderness. And the Bible says that the angel of the Lord appeared to her, and the angel of the Lord in the Old Testament was, Jesus Christ. Let me just say this again. Jesus came down and talked to our heartbroken, abandoned servant girl. Can someone just marvel with me at this part of the story, please?

When Jesus lived on this earth in the era of A.D., He did just that. He came to be close to the brokenhearted. It was prophesied about Him in Isaiah 61 and He fulfilled his mission on this earth, culminating with His self-surrender on the cross of Calvary. Oh, the riches and mercies of our God. How amazing and magnificent our Lord is.

And He spoke to her out there, telling her to return to her mistress and surrender to her. Jesus also told her that the baby she was carrying would be a "wild donkey of a man." I have to chuckle at the description. Our Ishmael was described like that? Ha, ha. She was also told that God would use her in His plan and she would be the mother of a great nation. Wow—simply, wow!

She called the name of the Lord in that moment and that time, Jehovah El Roy, the God who sees. And through the ages, He remained the same and this is one of His many names: Jehovah El Roy. So when accusations are being thrown at me, when I feel hands lifted up holding stones, I have decided that my only defense and reply will be—Jehovah El Roy.

My God sees. Yes, He does. My Jesus sees me, my situation, my circumstances, my pain, my brokenness, my desires, my tears. And He tells me: "Return to the place you have started from, the place of total surrender to the one who knows you, who loves you, and who wants to direct your life. Return to me, because I am a good Master."

"I am who I am, my Jehovah El Roy. I am here, Lord. Use me. Hineni!"

Letter to the Other Woman

You do not know me because we have never met. Yet, you were part of my life for so many years. I first saw you in a picture with Nick. He was holding you under his arm and both of you were smiling. A sharp knife-like pain penetrated my soul. The picture was taken in Paris.

I fell onto my knees. No, Lord, please, I can't deal with him having an affair . . . again, but curiosity overpowered me and I could not stop. In picture after picture I saw you—in Venice, in Switzerland, in Italy, at Tahoe on the beach with him, and later in my beautiful Romania. I took screen shots of course, not only to confront him, but to have time to study you.

When confronted of course, he used lame excuses. He said we were separated when he met you, though I would later find out that it was a lie. We were in the process of divorcing but forgetting that I never wanted this kind of relationship, I dropped the case and wanted nothing more than to work on our marriage.

I married him when I was not even twenty years old. He was my one and only. We have by this time been married over thirty years and more than anything else, I loved him. Oh, how I loved him.

These pictures were taken in 2018. I would need so much time and concentration to write about everything that happened from the time I saw you until I left him. Five years passed—five long and painful years.

Before I go any further, I would like you to know that today as I write this, I have totally forgiven you. Not because I was and am able to do it, but because the lover of my soul, the One who walked with me through these dark valleys, helped me. Because I was forgiven by Him, I can grant forgiveness to those who wronged me.

It was a very long process, but I can joyfully say that I have forgiven you, and I have so much peace and unbelievable freedom. I have forgiven you for taking my husband away from me and my children. I have forgiven you for being in a relationship with a married man. I have forgiven you for being in my home when I was not there and sleeping in many of my rooms and using my kitchen, my living space, totally disregarding that it was my sanctuary. I have forgiven you for the items of your personal effects that you have left behind, whether on purpose or not . . . I do not know.

I have forgiven you for traveling with my husband, even if you knew that he left me home to take care of our business, our children, our affairs, and his parents. I have forgiven you for the many holidays and New Year Eves that he had to run to you. I have forgiven you even though you knew he had elderly parents back home whom he ignored for so many years because of being so infatuated with you. I have forgiven you for being the "Other Woman!"

Now, may I ask you a few questions? I can? I hope you said yes. Okay, thank you. In the kindest way I know how, I would like to ask you: Did you ever have any remorse for living with Nick, knowing he was married? Did you ever think about the pain you have caused me? Do you know what it is like to see your husband leave with his pillows, blankets, and luggage, to spend time with his mistress?

And because I do not know what your answer is, allow me to say: I hope you will never know the pain and devastation Nick's betrayal brought me and our children. I hope you will never experience such deep despair that causes one to lose herself. Because I succumbed to such pits of depression, I wanted to end my life. It was never attempted, but I contemplated it. I loved him so much, I begged him to stay home and not go to be with you.

I tried to reason with him to see that our family was

worth fighting for. I hated you for having so much power over him, for he left after just receiving a text from you. You were his escape from reality, from the hard, pressing issues at home which he totally ignored, because "he had a girlfriend, "to which I always said, "A mistress." I thought about contacting you, but he always threatened me that if I did, he would leave me. Gaslighting is what he did, and so much more.

This is not a place where I unload my feelings on him and talk about the abuse he subjected me to for many years. No, I am dealing with him separately. I must, because the pain, if put collectively, is too much to bear.

So, I think I am about to finish my letter. I do not expect an answer. I do not know where you are in your relationship with him (although I know it has been broken) and am not sure if reconciliation happened or if he, as he is almost divorced, will run back to you. If he does it will hurt, but I won't suffer anymore.

I can honestly say that I do not hurt as much anymore. He now has the freedom to have you without any constraints, because he is no longer married to me. May the Lord bless you and keep you, may He shine His face upon and be gracious to you, and may He shine His countenance upon you and give you shalom.

Damaris, formerly Onofrei

P.S. Since I wrote this meditation, I found out that he ran back to her. Not unexpected. I hurt for a minute and then . . . I let go.

I Wonder if . . .

I wonder if his heart is tender,
To just miss me . . . for a bit.
For so many were the moments,
When he was my life, my lit.

And I wonder if his pillow,
In tears fills his lovely nights.
For mine was, and is my friendly,
Company enshrined in lights.

I still wonder if he misses,
My voice, and my tender touch.
For I shudder at the mem'ries,
And I miss him, oh so much!

And I wonder if our laughter,
Still creates in him a void.
And he misses me the same way,
Though it is now all destroyed.

I do wonder and I wonder,
Day and night, and night and day,
Does he . . . is he . . . did he,
will he . . .
Let his spirit fly away?

For to catch it would be going,
To a new and fresh begin.
Welled up though, my heart reminds me,
That it won't be as it's been.

So, in brokenness of spirit,
I lay down my life to Him.
Who is able to redeem me,
Who can wash away my sin!

And my wonders stop, and my heart,
Feels anew and fills with peace.
Supernatural for He is,
All I've longed for, and I've missed.

Hallelujah, my Redeemer,
Lives, thus I can live . . . again.
A new life filled to the fullest,
Glory to God and Amen.

January 6, 5:15 in the Morning, Home.

I got home about half an hour ago after having spent nine hours in jail. Yes, you read it right, I was in the Martinez County Jail. I have a lot on my mind so I will try to gather my thoughts to start from the beginning, to try to make sense of everything that transpired.

I left yesterday afternoon to get a sports massage at the physical therapy place where I had my legs worked on. It came highly recommended, and was something my lower extremities would need, considering that I still had a lot of problems with them. I was hoping that this kind of massage would alleviate some of the swelling and pain.

I had worked on my iPad all day, and I was quite frustrated because I couldn't make it work using my finger on the screen. I tried to connect the mouse but I was unable to, and though I did some research, but I still couldn't figure out how to do it.

I texted my son to let him know that I would be in the area that afternoon and to ask his father to return the iPad pencil that I gave him when he couldn't find his, and he had never returned.

The message came back very bluntly. He said, "You're not getting any pens from here so go buy a new one." That didn't sit well with me, to say the least.

I walked into the physical therapy place and when the massage therapist heard me coughing, he wanted to postpone my session. Despite my assurances that I was okay, he didn't feel comfortable. It was terribly disappointing because I was so looking forward to it. I texted my son again, to tell him that I would stop by the mailbox, where I asked him to kindly put my pencil along with any mail that I still had at my house, which was now inhabited by my estranged husband and my son.

He didn't text back, so I went to the house, parked my car on the lower part of the driveway, and called him. Six times I called him, but absolutely, no answer. So, because the garage door was up, I walked into the kitchen and that was my big mistake. Seeing some mail on the counter, I started to sort it, and that's when I saw Nick walking out of the bedroom yelling, "What are you doing here? You're not supposed to be here! Where is the police escort? You agreed not to come here," and on and on like that. He was yelling and he was furious.

I never "agreed" with any of that, and the police escort was forced upon me because like many times before, I told him that this is my home and I'm just here to collect a few things and then I'm going to leave. I asked for my iPad pencil and he said I couldn't have it. By this time, my son started recording it on his phone, of course, and he snatched the mail out of my hand.

Oh, I could not understand how this abuse was continuing after so many months of trying to get the attorney to put a stop to it or to get a restraining order, which she told me was hard to get, or to have a court date so the judge could look over our case and make the right decisions.

In my mind, Nick took the law into his own hands, again and again, and I was prohibited from going into either of my two homes. My militant spirit was very disturbed and my cry for justice was unheard. The mental, verbal, and emotional abuse was at an all-time high, and was physical many times too. And somehow, I had to give up everything because he said so.

What followed next was, of course, a verbal exchange, and I could hear Nick saying, "I can't believe you're here! I just can't believe you're here! Caleb, call Babu," (the nickname for my father).

"Please," I yelled. "Keep him out of this."

Then I heard by son on the phone with my father say: "Mom is acting crazy again.

Please come . . ."

No matter how much I yelled so my father could hear me, he didn't, and he showed up to "rescue" his daughter from the evil imposed on her. Jesus's voice sounded so close to me: "If you who are earthly, know how to give good gifts to your children, how much more your Father in heaven delights to bless those whom He loves."

At some point, standing in the middle of the hallway, I got on my phone to try to record him, but he snatched it and threw it outside into the mud. Past experiences flashed in front of my eyes; he has done this before, many times, and the thought of not having a phone again sent shivers down my spine. I started yelling, telling him he cannot do this, that the phone is my lifeline, and it's illegal, and he got even more verbally abusive and at some point, I hit him!

He immediately said, "I'm calling the police."

"Let's call the police, Dad, because she's abusing us!" my son chimed in.

What? I'm abusing, them? The abusers accusing the victim of the abuse they were rendering! What? And then right in front of me, Cale dialed the number and told his father to talk to them.

I was furious by this time. Not the police again. Having had a few encounters with them in the past when I was trying to report abuse and they did absolutely nothing about it, I had decided in my heart that I would never call them again unless I was half dead. To make a long story short, they came, and my father arrived about the same time.

"No, Dad, please don't come in. I don't want you to be privy to this scene!" I yelled.

Dad, his face ashen, his eyes humid, said, "Oh, my daughter . . . Oh, my daughter."

The policemen were very rude to me and had absolutely no compassion, no patience, and no tolerance for any of my exclamations, and I felt totally disrespected by them again. Misogyny is the word. Yes, I felt it again and again, every single time they were in my house. The battle of the sexes will never end, and the men will always win, sadly.

The officer that interviewed me grumpily agreed with me in the end. "Your son was not disciplined when he needed it," he said. "That's why he is abusive to you." A warm and a cold one. Gulp. "And your husband is not very nice, but I'm just doing my job," he said, trying not to show any normal human emotions.

Just doing his job! Cops. I don't know how to feel about them. Well actually, I do, and it's not good. The other officer, who took a long time to speak with my son and my estranged husband in the kitchen, came back and placed me under arrest!

I started to ask questions and he didn't like it. I asked him what was my charge and he said, "Domestic abuse."

I find it so unbelievably funny. Never mind that my counselor suggested that I call the abuse hotline and report that I was a victim of domestic abuse, but I had decided not to do that, thinking I would just let the attorneys do their job and get this horrific journey finished.

I had moved out of my house to get away from the abuse and the toxic environment. And today, they had the audacity to lie to the police and portray me as an unstable woman, an abuser, which warranted of course, a visit to the state penitentiary. The image I was left with as I was escorted out in handcuffs was a sneakered face, full of hate from Nick, and my son's face equally full of victory as he yelled out the words, "I hate you!"

And the face of my sweet father, bowed in defeat, succumbed to the pain of seeing his daughter led out of the home he had built, in handcuffs. I truly wondered if the demons had a dance party on my roof that night, snickering, seething, declaring victory, very proud of what their main followers had accomplished.

But I also wondered how heaven reacted. I used to sing a song called "Ten Thousand Angels Cried." Sometimes I do wonder if that would even be possible for these very powerful, heavenly beings. I don't think they have the emotions that human do.

In the back of the police car with my hands cuffed behind me, and my shoulders hurting because of the hunched over position, I felt an angel next to me.

"You are here," I whispered. "Right?" I felt that he had just nodded his head.

"I wouldn't let you go alone," he said. "Your little militant spirit got you in trouble again, huh?"

"Yup," I said. "I cannot stand the injustice. It's so wrong and so unfair."

"Do you not know that God will avenge you?" he said. "Why don't you wait?"

"How long will it be?" I asked, "because I don't have any patience left. I know He will, and I was told not to ask for his justice, but rather for His mercy."

"That's not a bad thought at all," the angel said.

"How many times did King David ask for justice in the Psalms, lamenting: "How long, how long until you will avenge your servant?" I challenged.

"You need to learn more patience," I heard him say, and my mind turned to just watching the car driving through my neighborhood down the street onto the freeway.

I have lived in this town for thirty years, and I am a law-abiding citizen. I never had any run-ins with the police. Never! And now, at the request of my son and estranged husband, I was being driven away to a prison. Damaris, the criminal. My hands were numb from the shackles and my right shoulder was starting to hurt. I was watching the streets go by from behind the grill in the police car. Me—the hands that nursed my son and wiped his tears. The hands that cooked his food and packed his lunches for school. The hands that wrote the checks for his tuition. Yeah, those hands were in handcuffs because they requested it! My son! My husband!

Tears were flowing abundantly and my leggings were absolutely soaked. Hard rock music was playing in the car with the volume cranked up. I could not follow the lyrics or the melody, but the following words I deciphered: "She stuck around for you . . ." How sadly fitting for my journey of the past five years. How sadly fitting.

I watched as exits went by—the exit to my new house, the exit to my brothers' homes, the exit to my parents' house. We were going to Martinez County Jail, but at some point I was lost to where we were. I was trying to take it all in, to make mental notes, to be aware of my surroundings. Tried to read boards or anything that would leave a lasting impression on me.

"Get out of the car," came a friendly voice (I'm being facetious). I thought to myself, "Can you try to get out when your hands are locked up behind you and the space is so tight?" But I've learned that to not say anything is better. The cops have no sympathy. They do not care. When you are in their custody, you have lost all your rights, I will come to find out later.

For a brief moment, I heard the cries from a black man handcuffed on the ground with a police officer's knee on his neck. And even though his cries were telling them he could not breathe, they did not stop until he stopped breathing (no pun intended). Police brutality is real and it's happening all around us. George Floyd, today you have earned my deepest sympathy.

What happened next was kind of a blur. I had to go to "check-in" where they strip you of everything you own. And while you wait to be fingerprinted, you are placed in a holding cell.

Let me try to describe it: blue floors, gray, uncomfortable chairs, yellow, dirty walls, red mirrored windows, two toilets, two pay phones, and many signs written in Spanish. I was trying to find some signs in English, but I couldn't find any. Hmm. Overall, very dirty and poorly kept.

There was also a big sign saying: "All inmates must be seated at all times." I did not obey that, and they didn't seem to care whether I was walking or sitting, because I knew they were watching me through those mirror windows. On the floor, the body of a woman was shaking and moaning.

"Lord," I whispered. "Am I really here in prison? I'm being called an inmate, for real?

I sat down and I started to pray, and an unbelievable peace came over me. "Start worshiping," I heard a voice say, and worship I did. I sang all the songs that came to mind, like "Amazing Grace," and "Oh the Blood of Jesus," and "I Love You Lord," and "To God be the Glory," and "Blessed Assurance."

My voice was still raspy from the laryngitis but was resounding throughout the prison. My hands were lifted up high and I didn't care who heard me because I knew the presence of the Lord was there. And strangely, the man who was yelling from down the hallway when I first walked in, became quiet. The lady on the floor said to me, "Please, continue to sing. "I like it!"

I learned that she was a homeless person who was arrested for stealing food. She was so sick. I think she had pneumonia. Of course, she did. She lived under the freeways. She was shaking with fever and I tried to get the nurse to come over and do a medical assessment and give her some medication. But they yelled at me through the door: "We're busy now, we don't have time."

Of course they are!

I took my long black duster and I wrapped it around her. I took her in my arms and I started to rub her back, her hands, her head, and immediately she rested her head on my shoulder, held onto my hand, and fell asleep. I found it ironic that I was on my way to get a massage and now in a prison holding cell, I was comforting and massaging the back of a very broken and lost, beautiful, young woman.

I told her stories about Jesus and I sang to her. I think she just needed the love of a mother, so for a brief moment, she relaxed and felt safe. "Oh, Lord," I whispered. "I have a nice home and a clean bed to go home to, but how about Cordelia?" That was her name.

In the prison holding cell that night I met three other women that were booked for domestic abuse, all three reporting the same familiar story—abusive husbands requesting their arrest because they stood up and had the guts to defend themselves. Only when one walks this road one understands. I met Susan, I met Lacey, and I met Linda, all beautiful women, now at the mercy of cruel and unforgiving police officers. Bullies with guns—that's what they are! There is so much injustice in this world, Lord. So much injustice.

After I got photographed and fingerprinted, I thought, "Good job, Damaris. Now you have a new they-fie." (just made up the word—a picture taken by them, the police). Good job!"

"May I please wash my hands?"

"No."

"Sit down on that bench?"

"No rights."

I am being treated like a criminal. Is this what happens to the innocent until proven guilty?

"Not here. Nope. Not here. Now sign here, here, and here," a rough officer said.

"Sir, I'd like to read what I am signing."

"Just sign."

"Nope, I will read it first!"

They did not like me. Oh well. I understood that I was not here to make an impression on them. They told me that I could post bail and they would release me to my home. Thank you, Lord.

"How much longer," I asked?

"Four-to-six hours. Stop asking questions, Damaris. Just wait."

Back in the cell, I started to worship my God again and all the women gathered around me. So I led the first worship service in many long years here in a prison cell, along with my fellow inmates. I told the Lord I didn't think I wanted to be a worshipper on a church stage anymore.

"Well, here you go," He seemed to say. "I'll give you a prison platform."

"I'm okay with this, Lord," because His peace was so prevalent there. Unbelievable peace—there, in prison. Everyone had time to share their stories, and I was allowed to share the gospel, the sweet message of salvation, the love of a Savior, the only love which does not disappoint. The only one whose love is so amazing, He would never ask for his creation to be put in jail." Heads nodded, amens erupted, and my mission was accomplished.

I was the first one to be released. "Can she stay a bit longer?" they asked the police officer.

"Sorry girls, but I am going home!"

Released on bail at three o'clock in the morning, the burdened face of my dear father met me outside. He took me to his home where Mom awaited me with warm soup and cozonac, which is Romanian for walnut roll. The sweet aroma of home overwhelmed me. What about those who don't have a home and family to go back to? Lord . . . You are so, so, good.

Back home, nestled in my comfy bed and surrounded by my two sweet doggies, I whispered, "Lord, there are many lessons you need me to learn from here. But right now, after the shock wore off just a little bit, I am just thankful that your presence was with me. Thankful that I could impart the message of salvation with those sweet women whose faces will be forever etched in my memory. I will never forget this. I will not let this experience go to waste. Use me, Lord, as you teach me to walk humbly with You, because all my soul desires are for you to be glorified even from such an experience as this.". Then I whispered the following words: "Sola Scriptura, Sola Fide, Soli Deo Gloria," and I fell asleep.

On Good Friday, I Am Asking for Justice

When in contrast, Jesus was punished so, we can be forever with God. Lord, You were lonely on the cross and I too am lonely today. You see and you know. You've been there, within, without them, but with us in mind, with me on Your mind. Oh, how I love you. I am not alone. You will go before me, You will never leave me. The perfect Son of God was treated as a criminal.

Lord, I know I am being mocked. Yet when You were, You did not open your mouth. Falsely accused, You remained silent. Lord, Lord, help me follow suit. It's hard to be silent. It's hard, Lord. Their eyes were closed. They did not see. They blindfolded Jesus when they themselves were blind. The Son of God was standing in front of them. Yet, they did not see. He experienced brutal suffering. Isaiah 53. Prophetic. He saw thousands of years before it happened.

Nothing beautiful about His appearance. Yet, He was the most beautiful of men. It was our sorrows that weighed Him down. Pierced, beaten, whipped, crucified, nails in His feet and hands, thorns on His head. He was struck, spit on, mocked. How did you stay silent, Lord?

I am asking for justice today, but you did not. You were pierced for my sins. You did not ask for justice. No . . . No . . . No. You took it all, for me. The shadow of death. The Passover lamb. Perfect. Exodus 12:21-23. Slathering the Passover lamb, the blood will save you and your family. So, they put it on their door post, so the destroyer will not enter your house and strike you down.

I am thirsty. Vinegar. It is finished . . . the pain of being hung on the tree . . . such pain. Will any of us know? Never! He gave up His Spirit.

Sprinkle my heart with Your precious blood. Wash me clean tonight. Do not pass me by. For I have been already passed by the destruction and punishment.

Lord, I am so thankful. I am so thankful. Nothing but the blood of Jesus. Saturday was the silent day, but then, Sunday came. And for that, I am overwhelmed with gratitude.

I Carry You in My Spirit

I pray for you more than I pray for myself. I stayed and longed for you. I served you and treated you as my husband, minus your love. No matter—I stayed. But one day, God called me out of the grave and put my feet on solid ground again. So . . . I will let you go, Nick. You will never know how deeply I loved you. My Redeemer lives! And because He lives, I can say tomorrow.

I do wish you well, but no, I won't and can't be in your life. It will take a long time to heal. And I will never love again the way I loved you.

Your Ex-Wife

P.S. You will get your bifurcation of status and will be single soon. Take the kids out and celebrate. Single and divorced, you have accomplished your dream. For I, will never be the same again. Never!

Even in the Valley, He is with Me, and I will Fear No Evil

Because this long and painful journey is ending, evil intensifies. The enemy knows that he's lost his grip on me—on my mind, heart, and soul—because he came to destroy and he thought he won! But . . . God. But . . . God. What the enemy meant for evil, God, is turning into good. What Nick wanted to destroy, we got to build new.

In Isaiah chapter 61-3, we read that God will raise beauty

out of ashes. Yes, He does! And I am a living testimony! I can and I will always testify about the goodness of God! I will always sing. I will always worship Him, because He and only He is worthy.

Yesterday was December 4, 2022. I have moved most of my stuff from my marital home into the rental, much to Nick's displeasure, and of course my son's. The moving company arrived around 9:30 a.m. and the whole previous night from midnight to five in the morning, Nick wanted to talk to me. I did not want to sit in the same room with him, but he insisted because we truly have not talked for many months.

Our *talk* was not a normal talk. Not what anybody would consider a normal conversation. No, because we trigger each other. Because the hatred in his heart was so deep, for five hours he just vomited anger! I cannot say that I did not react to his accusations, which I have heard over and repeatedly. I did try to reason with him, reasonably (no pun intended). I did yell and scream, telling him repeatedly that all I want is my freedom. That I want out! That this house is toxic That I cannot and will not stay here anymore.

I told him that I am moving out, partially because I do not trust him. He was very angry about things that I already took out of the house, like some of my pictures, some art, some dishes, glasses, coffee cups, and of course one of my pianos, my beautiful upright Yamaha which I relocated to my parents' house. He was mad. He was beyond mad. He destroyed things in the house because of it—yelling and screaming—because I did not ask his permission, and I did not *communicate*!

So, that morning when the moving people came, he was ready with the phone set on record, sitting behind the glass door in the kitchen and constantly yelling, "Thief!"

We made it out of the house okay, and then we unloaded at the new rental. And I saw myself pictured in this image: from my house on the hill in beautiful Lafayette, to the house in the valley in a new town, unfamiliar to me.

Lord, the Psalms are full of laments and cries for You to walk with King David, on the mountain tops but also in the valleys.

Almost picture perfect to the circumstances of my life, today.

So, again in an attitude of total surrender I cry out to Him and say:

As you were faithful to your servant of the old, so you will be to me, oh God of my salvation!

As you walked with him, many times in his valleys, you will walk with me. You will be my strength, my portion, my rock, my refuge.

In You I trust and patiently wait to see how things will unfold.

I love you, Lord! I truly do love you deeply!

"For we do not wrestle against flesh and blood . . ." Ephesians 6:12

It is very rainy and cold outside. This is winter in California and I'm so grateful for the rain because I enjoy it. It's much needed for our vegetation and for all of the reservoirs. I know here and there because of the heavy rains there are floods and mudslides but overall, the freshness that comes after a good rain cannot compare with anything else.

I do enjoy walking in the rain, providing that I have the

proper gear on, because no, I do not like to be wet, because I don't think I can any longer afford it at my age. No singing in the rain for me and Mr. Fred Astaire. But I don't mind driving in the rain because I do have a good car for which I'm grateful.

Last night I was invited by my mother to come over for dinner, but I politely declined. I had a lot on my mind. Had a lot to do at home so I just cooked myself a very simple dinner of rice and vegetables. After dinner, as I was closing the window to my living room, I saw a young man walking up to my front door. He was holding a bunch of papers in his hand, and my heart started to beat fast. Oh no, it has arrived.

He called my name. He asked me if I was Mrs. Onofrei and he just handed me a pack of papers, serving a restraining order from my now estranged husband. My heart sank, because I was informed by my attorney that he would do that, and to expect it.

Well, for a moment I thought I should have accepted my mother's dinner invitation so I would not have been home for an event such as this, my understanding being that this kind of paperwork has to be handed to the person directly.

"It doesn't matter," I thought, because I would've been served at a different time anyway. I sat on my sofa in the living room and after I wiped away tears, I opened the package.

Page after page, I read false statements about my life, my behavior, who I am, or maybe I should say who I was perceived to be by them—my own family—my husband, my son, and my in-laws. Totally false, painting pictures of me that were unsettling. Many, many, untruthful statements.

"Lord," I cried out again. "On top of everything else, now this?" I had a restraining order to attend to in a criminal court (due to my arrest) and now this is one from the civil court? I need you so much right now, Lord.

I sat at the piano and I sang. I worshiped Him through many tears. Despite all, despite all, He is worthy. He is on His throne, and nothing is out of his control.

Made some phone calls, and then sat down again. Remembering the verses in Ephesians 6:12 well, too well, I whispered: "For we war not against flesh and blood, but against the powers, the principalities, the spiritual forces of evil in the heavenly places, the demons, whose only mission is to kill, steel, and destroy."

The next morning, I was going to have a meeting with a new attorney since mine was going to opt out soon. I went to bed and fell asleep praying. And as I woke up, my spirit was calm. My sister arrived early in the morning for a weekend getaway, and she called me after she arrived at my parents' home.

"How are you, Sis? We are praying alongside you," she said. "Go in the favor of the Lord."

As I was getting ready, I called my friend Marleen. Her prayers erupted from the other end of the phone, prayers of bonding the enemy, prayers of declaring victory, and prayers asking for God's will to be done.

As I was driving to the office attorney's office, I called Donna, my other friend who is equally gifted and trained to fight the spiritual war. I asked her to pray for me and the first question out of her mouth was, "Have you put on your armor today?"

"No, I have not," I said, "so let's do it together."

A chorus of praises and hallelujahs went up to the throne of grace and equipped with His armor we asked for mercy and grace, kindness and victory, restraint of the enemy, and opened doors.

How amazing that I was covered by my family first, and then by two beautiful godly friends, Dana and Marleen, ages eighty-eight and ninety, respectively. Oh Lord, you are so good. You are so, good!

I tried not to cry too much because I didn't want to ruin my makeup. My spirit was edified, and I knew that I knew that heaven and the answer to the prayer was on its way. With that confidence, I walked into my meeting with the new attorney.

Isn't our Lord just too amazing? Yes, He is. Glory Hallelujah!

Make Their Stoning Not Hurt Anymore, Lord

Nothing is concealed from Your eyes, Lord. You see, You know, You cover, Your blood saves, You forgive and forget. But not them. They wait for a moment of weakness, for a slip. They sit in waiting for the prey to fall to the ground with stones in their hands—ready. The words hurt. Their words hurt. They kill.

You are . . . and you do . . . you need to . . . my beautiful children casting stones. My handsome husband, full of hatred, calling me all kinds of names. Accusing with a knifed tongue, meant to hurt . . . and kill. Yeah, to kill.

My mind goes to the woman thrown at the feet of Jesus. I could hear their accusations because through the ages and times past, they find their way into our lives. Don't you agree? Sinner! Deserving of death! With their hands up and ready, with their fingers clutching their stones, they await His verdict. And He just writes in the sand. So amazing of the Lord. They wait, and He writes.

Allowing them to boil. Surely, He knows, if He indeed is the prophet He claims to be. He knows, He sure does. He knows their hearts too—full of hatred and righteousness and sinfulness? Is there such a thing? Well, there is now, and I can just imagine how gently but firmly He told them: "Let he who has no sin cast the first stone," and continued to write.

Who knows how much time passed? What we know is that after a while, He looked up and asked: "Woman, where are your accusers?"

"They left, Lord" her voice filled with fear, replied.

And He pronounced the verdict that every person alive today and through the ages longs to hear: "If they don't condemn you, neither do I. Go in peace, but sin no more."

Can you hear it, my family? Can you? But my question is not heard because, it falls on deaf ears. Because I am supposed to live without shortcomings. "You are controlled by your emotions," they tell me. "In fact, you have been emotionally unstable all my life," my oldest child said to me. Sent shocks through my body. All her life? Is this how she feels? Is she right? No, she can't be. All . . . her . . . life?

"Take care of your life, Mom. You're an adult," and the door slammed. And it left a vibrating echo through my entire body, mind, and soul. "Take care of yourself. Get help. You need it!"

My daughter . . . my daughter . . . I need your arms around me. I thought you were going to walk with me along this road less traveled. I don't know how to manage sharing you, dividing our family, our things, renting a place when for so many years I owned my home. A home, or should I say homes, which I now need to let go of, to give to others to enjoy. My daughter, please don't leave me . . . I need you.

My pleas were met by a stony heart. My voice echoed back through the empty house. My daughter . . . oh, my daughter . . . my sweet, sweet, Adrianne. If you could just turn for a moment and look back—your mama wants to hold you close, to not let go of you. Could you please come back for just a moment?

Silence . . .

Will he ever know how desperately I loved him? How much I longed for him? How I watched him from behind always loving his body? Manly, not muscular, but lean. Long hair now curly. Watching him walk away, knowing full well that he was leaving to be in the arms of another. Will he ever know the pain he caused me? I don't think so.

Would he also know how desperately painful it was to see him walk in the house after he'd spent time away with her? Always smelling so good because he always used cologne when he visited her. Always! I loved it and hated it! She got to hold him close to her and take in his beautiful body, smelling so amazing.

I hated her many times. Many times! She was "allowed" to put her fingers through his hair, but I was not. She was allowed to touch him, but I was not, and if I did, I was told it was not appropriate.

"Mom, stop throwing yourself at Dad. It shows desperation and it's not attractive," my son would say.

"Oh, Caleb. I don't know how to let him know that I still want him."

"Not like this, Mom," he would say. "Not like this."

And he was right. After all, we were separated, and he had a girlfriend. Did I not get this? Has he not been with her for years? Yes, indeed . . . he has. What in the world? How come we all talked and accepted this? My children were okay with their father being in another relationship. I wanted to scream, and I did many times, "Is this okay with you? Don't you care that he has another family? This is so crazy!"

"Please, Nick," I would beg. "Come home, baby."

He called her babe. I know because I broke the code to his phone and I voraciously read through the messages. It was painful. It was crazy, and the more it hurt, the more I wanted to know. And like a masochist, I continued to dig deep into my heart with a knife.

He was in love with her. At least that is what it looked like. She was his sunshine, his beautiful girlfriend. She was worthy, he told her, of the best life could offer. He took her to Paris, Italy, Switzerland, Romania, and many places in America where beauty was on display. Because after all, she deserved.

As I'm writing these hard, hard, truths, my heart bleeds yet again—bleeds because I desired to be his copilot, to be his companion on those trips. Instead, she was by his side. She sat next to him in the beautiful Mercedes or BMW he rented for them.

Yeah, it hurts, and I know it will always hurt to visit these memories . . . always. Are all wives in this world like me? Holding on for so long? Suffering so much? And right about now, I do not know the answer.

But what I know for sure if this:

Whether the stoning will continue or not, my prayers have been answered. It is beginning to not hurt as much and I know that one day, when healing will be complete, I will be able to confidently say: Through it all, He was my refuge, the place where I hid and found respite.

For all of us women who have walked or are walking this road, as a sojourner with you I will say: Take heart, you will overcome, through Him.

I am living testimony and so will you be.

Some Have Bucket Lists . . .
Some Have Buckets of Tears . . .

As I'm sitting in my living room looking out the window this beautiful fall morning, my gaze is transfixed upon the beautiful trees. Surrounded by old oaks, our house stands high up on the hill. It was named "The house on the hill" for a reason.

Fall is my favorite season. I love the changing of colors, the dropping of leaves, and walking through trails full of rusty leaves. I love the noise our boots make dancing around them. Yet, while looking at this beauty, so many images are scrolling through my mind. I almost see myself actually not even walking, but just moving slightly above the earth with the peace that only the Holy Spirit can give, touching as I move, different people's lives.

My mind goes back to Romania, the county I was born in. And even though I've lost connection with it, I have reacquainted myself with it in the last few years. Funny how a world pandemic can change people's lives. I am not referring to the land itself, but to something more amazing—to godly, God-fearing people.

So many names, so many needs, my mind tries to remember whom we prayed for, for the last two-to-three years: Liuta, Ezme, Mircea, Benjamin, Tobias, Dorotea, Salomia, Gabi, Stefania, Florentina, Beatrice, Simona, Voichita,

Elena, Carmen, Lorena, Cristina. Aaagh—so many needs, so many needs. Oh, but God . . . God knows them all.

Without realizing it, my mind goes back to my situation. Still walking in the War Zone, still fighting, but not against flesh and blood, but against the powers and principles of the dark forces in the heavenly realms, which descended upon my house and have inhabited some members of my family. Ephesians 6:12.

I was reminded recently that people make bucket list. Lists, if you wish, that they try to fulfill as they live through life, as if to say at the end: Look what I have done and where I've been. I have done this, and this, and this. I went there, and there, and there. Check. Check. Check. Bucket lists.

But the image that I have for myself is of buckets full of tears. Still buckets, but filled with tears. All kinds of tears, of course. Tears of pain, tears of fear, tears of surrender, tears of joy, tears of happiness, tears of sadness, tears of amazement, tears of awe, tears of excitement, tears over God's beautiful creation, tears of abandonment, tears over the amazingness of God, tears of desperation, tears of loneliness, and even tears that come after something gets into your eyes. Yeah, tears, tears, tears . . . buckets of tears.

I often thought that I would not be able to produce any more tears. I thought that I filled enough buckets, without remembering that our eyes produce them every single day, that yes, we are capable of crying for long periods of time and the process can be repeated each and every single day of our lives.

As I'm getting ready to go about my day, as I meditate at God's goodness and mercy today, I am crying tears of thankfulness. And boy do I have things to be thankful for. Yes, I do. And I am mentally making lists of them in my head right now.

Would you join me? The journey is hard, but I promise it will be rewarding. Let's get started. Thank you and shalom!

As the Water Rages, the Calmer I Am

I'm beginning to understand why God said in the *Book of Micah* that he hates divorce. Many people think, or the common understanding is, that God hates divorce because it is a break of a covenant, a covenant made between a husband and a wife in front of God. Especially for the believers.

And I know that God takes it very seriously. He definitely hates breaking of the "one flesh" because breaking of ONE flesh hurts! And if it hurts us, I am pretty sure that it hurts the heart of God. I'm sure he also hates divorce because of what it does to the people involved. It breaks the family apart and it separates parents from children, daughters from in-laws, sons from mothers, and so on. It is pure evil, because the author of divorce is not God, but Satan himself. Of course, he comes to instigate, he comes to separate, he comes to destroy!

And without a doubt, it is also the fault of the husband and wife who do not stand watch, do not act in wisdom, do not know how to forgive, do not know how to stand firm, and do not know how to guard against the evil!

So I find myself in the midst of pure evil circumstances. The fact that my husband is capable of doing what he's doing leaves me asking, "How can one who once loved me be capable of such evil? How can one who was supposed to protect love and cherish do a 180? Mental games, emotional abuse, harassment, dismissal, sarcasm, nonchalance, whistling instead of being concerned, turning the back, walking away, threatening, and calling out accusations. Yes, divorce is evil, and it breaks anyone and everyone.

Dams are being formed, people take sides, emotions, brokenness, broken hearts, mental exhaustion, and the inability to think straight. This translates into all kinds of organic issues, illness, and emotional and physical distress. Need I continue? Have I painted a clear enough picture of a divorce? Can I scream it from the top of my lungs and post it on all the billboards across America and across the world for everybody who is considering divorce to stop and ponder? I sure wish I could!

I know I did everything humanly possible and otherwise for my family not to be a statistic. But in the end, he made his decisions and remains firm. "I do not have what it takes to be married to you!" he said, and with this he walked away!

Lord, if you will not be on my side, and if I cannot hide in the shadow of your wings, surely this disaster will overtake me! Surely the enemy will try to bring the destruction to the maximum. Surely, he might think that he has won the war! But you, oh God, are my shield and you, oh God, are my refuge! You are Jehovah El Roi. You are Jehovah Nissi. I don't know . . . I don't know! I love you most high God. I lean on the verse from Exodus chapter 14, verse 14-15, which says: "Fear not, stand firm and see the salvation of the Lord . . . the Lord will fight for you, and you have only to be silent . . ."

Hallelujah. "The Lord is my shepherd. I shall not want. He makes me lie down in green pastures. He leads me inside still waters. He restores my soul."

I Have Been Promoted
(Written on Saturday, August 19)

Last night was one of the hardest evenings of my life. It started well, with me communicating with him about stuff at the business. He even complimented me on a job well done. I was there for an hour or so, taking care of some of my beautiful residents. I moved with ease from room to room, working effortlessly to change beds—to touch and comfort minds which were not in touch with reality, as we know it. I had one more to do. I took care of two. I had to sit because I could not catch my breath.

"Lord," I cried. "What is going on? What is this? Still so dyspneic with exertion. How can I continue? Will you heal me from this? Send me to the right doctors?"

Okay, one more to check. My mother-in-law was with me. At her advanced age she was there willing and ready to help. But where are the caregivers? I looked at the time. It was 9:30 p.m. It's okay, they are resting. You can do this. You have to, and you have help. Sweet, sweet, Helen. What an amazing human being.

I walked into Julie's room. "Julie? *Comon va tue c'est-à-Nuie?*" I asked in my very limited French. And she replied, "*Je suis très bien.*" Oh, she still remembers. She spoke French in her early years. "I'm here to help you and check your skin."

"Okay," she said.

What followed was a total redoing of her bed—assessing and dressing some stage three closed pressure wounds. I don't know why and how I talked to my mother-in-law about him and lamented about my storm. I know I mentioned some personal stuff in lieu of us (me and her) having had a conversation the night before about abuse—stuff that happens in Christian homes. Horrible, covered, painful. I don't even know why I said what I said:

"When I remember that he slept with another woman, and for that long, I am sick to my stomach. " She looked at me with so much pain in her eyes.

Other things were said about the caregivers not always doing a good enough job. But when we left Julie to go back to sleep, I left all I said, in that room. I wanted to get home. By this time, it was just past ten o'clock. Believe me, when I left for home that evening, my mind was not even connected to that discussion.

I took my two dogs, the third being in the car this whole time, because she is like that.

My Lily always refuses to disembark for the fear of being left behind. Separation anxiety? I really don't know.

Fast forward later this evening in my conversation with Nick; he pulled out the guns. He saw and listened to all the conversations. Did I forget that there are cameras everywhere?

Yes, I did! And with that video he was out to kill—to destroy, to mar.

Lord, what is happening? And like a gong, like a church bell which still rings but is heard less and less, my whole being was going numb. Bong . . . Bong . . . Bong . . . Bong.

Lord, what is happening? And like a breath of fresh air, I've heard these words: This will never end. This . . . Will . . . Never . . . End! The name calling, the stoning, the um-humming of past sins, my failures, my mistakes, my lacks in judgement. All again on display for me to be reminded why we are here and why he left.

And right there and then I wanted, for the last time, to defend myself. I yelled and screamed as if to make him understand that I stayed for five years because I loved him. He knew that, because I told him so many times. And as he did a million or more times before, he dismissed me. My love. That was my choosing. He never asked. He told me where he was, and from the top of his lungs he screamed back, "Nothing has changed!"

What followed was the discovery from God Himself. My daughter, my sweet, sweet, daughter. I want you to quit your striving. Rest in me. You can't change him. Have you not tried? Yes, Lord. I did.

Today you have been promoted. Lord, you saw what just happened here. You, saw ! I did, and it grieved my heart. My daughter, I have other plans for you. The promotion is to a new level of a walk with me. Watch and see what I will do for you. Trust and obey, rest and believe, quit and let me do my work.

Yes, Sir . . . Lord . . . Master . . . Jesus. Yes!

Addendum:

Only two days after this, as I spend time talking to Him and asking Him for guidance, two of my very big issues were answered the same day. He guided me to find my home church, and He sent me my new attorney who will help me navigate my life to clean, safe waters.

Yeah, God is that good, because He told me to watch and see. And from where I'm standing right about now, it's looking pretty darn good. You are an awesome, awesome God! And the new song that I've just started to sing it's called: "The Goodness of God."

I love You, Lord, for Your mercy never fails me. All my

days, I've been held in Your hands. From the moment that I wake up until I lay my head down. Oh, I will sing of the goodness of God!

Meditations

I have been regurgitated on the shore of life from the belly of despair—severe pain, self-inflicted wounds, idolatry, and stubbornness, and it feels good to breathe clean air. I almost don't know what to do with the newfound freedom. No more swimming in murky waters, no more coming up for breath only to go down again to find my way swimming in the darkness.

For many years, I've had a recurrent dream: I was always swimming in the dark ocean, always trying to get to shore and never making it. It felt like I was in those nightmares very often in my sleep. I wonder now if the enemy of my soul did not try to put thoughts in my mind. There was so much darkness. There were always cold, windy, lonely nights.

But, to say that I've been rebirthed, is a total understatement. Like the prophet of the Old Testament, I too had run away from God, trying to find my own way, trying to figure life out on my own foolish wisdom, telling God what I need and what He should do for me, especially in the last decade of my life I should say. Even when at the Wailing Wall in Jerusalem I have heard His voice say: "Let go of your nonsense, because I will restore you and your relationships."

Even after He had given me a song called "Freedom", right there on the shores of the Sea of Galilee, and I have known and experienced His presence on the Temple Mount and walking on the empty streets of the City of David during Shabbat. And even then, I still asked Him how to intervene, how to change his life, how to cause things to happen, how to make him come back. Oh . . . the audacity of the creation, the nerve of a created being to tell her maker how to mold and sculpt her . . . the audacity.

But He, in His splendor and beauty, in His majesty and love, cared enough to reach down and say: "Let me know when you've had enough. Let me know when I can start the process. Because there is much to do, to make you into the image of my Son, because then and only then you will shine and reflect the Gospel of Salvation to the lost world around you."

In humility of spirit, in the locked chambers of my home, I surrendered fully, again and again. For life under His authority, is worth living.

TRAVELINGS

The Unimaginable Beauty of the South

I have lived in America for almost forty years, but I didn't do too much travelling to the East Coast. I mostly traveled up and down the West Coast and a little bit into the Midwest, and I have never ventured into the South.

The call came from my very best friend D who said: "I am going to Charleston. Now would be a good time for you to come." I did not have to think too hard or too long. My dear soul sister Emily helped me get a ticket and I found myself on the plane to Charleston, South Carolina. I was excited to see what God had prepared for me on this five-day journey.

I arrived safely and I found myself surrounded by such beautiful nature, my soul was immediately overwhelmed. "Lord," I said, "you are the Creator of such amazing beauty. Lord, you have given us so much to delight in."

The house that hosted me was a beautiful mansion. Nestled in a forest, it provided such a sanctuary for the body, mind, and soul. I was to embark on a retreat for total restoration because today, as I sit in the den enjoying my last few hours here, my soul is full, my body rested, and my spirit refreshed.

I don't even know where to begin to describe how the Lord spoiled me on this long weekend. So much to say, so much to describe, so overwhelmed with joy. I'll start by saying the vegetation here is magnificent. Luscious trees, plants, and grass surround each house. People here do not have fences. I guess the friendliness of the South helped people not to build constraining, property-defying fences.

The homes here are typically built of brick and sometimes have a structure that resembles the plantation style. I will not get into the history of the South in this meditation, as it will be a lot to say, and it will defeat the purpose of my writing at this time.

The sounds of nature in the South are musically rich: the birds, the crickets, the rain, the thunder, the ocean waves, the seagulls, other insects I do not know the names of, and oh, the church bells—lots of them. I prayed for rain and God answered because it rained every day. Oh, how I loved to hear it. I slept with my window open to fall asleep to its music. Even the gutters leaking noise was welcomed. At home, I occasionally listen to the sound of rain on my phone, but this was all natural. Ah, the freshness of the air, the smell of the fresh grass—nothing compares.

Our host was so gracious to take us to visit this historic city (another mutual friend was there with us). We went to Sullivan Island, which I was told had some of the most expensive real estate in the country. There on the beach, I tasted the salt water on my skin and I fed the seagulls chips and cookies. And boy did they cause a scene. Some were fighting over them and more and more came for the free snacks.

We went downtown where the architecture and the colors of the buildings left me aghast. Teal is the preferred color for the city, and it looked like all windows had baskets of flowers underneath. And next to teal I saw red roofs, yellow, white, green, and blue homes, and cobblestone streets covered by the meeting tree crowns. I played photographer and enjoyed every moment. The angel oaks with the weeping moss were a picture to behold. Never in my life have I seen such big trees with branches touching the ground. Most likely there for hundreds of years, they could tell stories, I'm sure. Beautiful boutiques were visited by beautifully dressed people. What is this place? A gathering of old class and beauty? Street after street of beautiful churches with tall spires. I was told no building can be taller than the church towers. Now this says a lot about this community. Loved to see that people still have a pious attitude, a respect for the Creator, a worshipful heart. I was slowly falling in love with the South.

I chuckled when I saw a shop called "Insomnia Cookies," and one called "Walking IV spa."

I mean the Southern belles need their beauty sleep and their skin maintained after all. And because I wanted to also taste the South, I enjoyed for the first time, fried tomatoes, and fried chicken and waffles—a strange combination but quite good.

In all this amazement, the Lord came down to listen to His three daughters worship and adore Him. I think the scroll of heaven rolled just enough for the angels to look, listen, and marvel. Because they will never understand the song of the redeemed and never will they taste the sweet sound of freedom. Never. Because they have no sin and thus no need for a Savior. They heard the voice say: "Here I am, send me," and ever since The Cross they fought for the blood of the Lamb and for the saints. Always on a mission, always ready to be dispatched when not in worship at the throne.

And they smiled when they smelled the aroma, the fragrance of the prayers being lifted, being deposited at the throne of grace. For protection, for direction, for discernment, for restoration, for grace and mercy, for open doors, doors to be closed, and for homes and families. Oh how they loved to tarry to see them until the end. As with hands on their swords and wings spread wide, they stand ready. And inside, basking in the peace that only Jesus can give, slept three tired warriors.

Meeting with the King in the Field

This is such a peaceful place. The wind is gently blowing and it is not hot. Just the perfect temperature. Around me, a myriad of names: James, Stuart, John, Elisabeth, Haley, Paul, Marcus—all on tombstones. Silk flowers adorn the ground for the most part and here and there fresh flowers, now wilted. No other noise but the sound of birds singing and an occasional airplane flying overhead.

And the voice of Jesus resounding through the ages: "I am the resurrection and the life. Whoever believes in Me shall never die."

What a conundrum. Sitting on this pasture filled with many loved ones of many people. I wonder—I try to understand. Death is the last enemy to be defeated, the Bible says. And Jesus did, when He rose from the dead and went up to the Father, from where He will again return, at the end of the ages.

It is good to ponder at life, because Scriptures also says that life is but a vapor—here today, gone tomorrow. Like the grass of the field—alive in the morning, gone by the evening. Hmmm. Sitting here, the words of Jesus stir up my heart. Unless you are born again, you will surely not inherit the kingdom of God.

Birth and death. It is what characterizes all humanity. We are all born into this life and all of us will die one day. We did not choose to be here. I guess you can say our parents did, although many times it came as a surprise for them too. But being born into the kingdom of God by faith in Jesus' sacrifice, is something that we can all choose. It's a choice for all. Living our lives preparing for eternity is what makes this earthly existence worth living. No puns intended. Walking among the stones, I saw the ages of the buried, from one day, to many decades. All here. I'm sure they left behind many fulfilled and unfulfilled dreams, many accomplishments, many failures, many victories, and many losses. And most heartbreaking, many loves ones.

I know someone who likes to always quote from Ecclesiastes: ". . . all is vanity and a chase after the wind . . ." And while it's true, I certainly would rather quote the verse that says: ". . . fear God and keep his commandments . . ."

Because in the end of it all, life has purpose because of Him. Life is rich when we walk in obedience to him, and when we fulfill our destiny here on this site of heaven. Because we also know that when the trumpet sounds and when His voice calls us, we all will leave this abode to be forever with Him.

I cannot wait to behold His glory. To bend my knee and worship Him, whose Spirit is even here, among the tombs, because He is ever present. Oh how sweet it is to trust in Jesus.

And as I'm about to get back to my car after my encounter with Him today, I start singing:

When the roll is called up yonder
When the roll is called up yonder
When the roll is called up yonder
When the roll is called up yonder
I'll be there

It's starting to drizzle gently . . .

Chicago is Where Our Story Began

Flying into Chicago, accompanied by my father and brother, my heart was excited. Though the event was a celebration of life for one of our cousins, who went home to be with the Lord, I was looking forward to seeing the city where I began life in America. Chicago, December 18th,1985, we descended into O'Hare Airport—two parents accompanied by eight children, all ages nineteen and down, the youngest being under one years old.

We arrived with so much joy in our hearts because we had escaped the communist regime from our motherland. America, the land of the free, the land of opportunities. America the beautiful, America the land craved by so many, was now our home.

I remember how happy I was going to school having just seventy-five cents in my pocket, enough to buy me a bag of chips and a Coke. I was hooked on that junk. I am sure it was because it was food we had not tasted before. And please somebody tell me, why does junk food taste so good? I have since relinquished this right to just consume, especially since I know how bad it is for my health.

We were living the dream, and we never took anything

for granted. Being a child of an immigrant, I was taught early on that we needed to work hard. My parents were and will remain my role models. Our beginnings in Chicago were extremely modest: Irving park, Harlem, Belmont, Cicero, Diversey and Central, Diversey and Long Street.

But our time in the windy city was short. After only couple of years, we relocate to California.

My father made that decision for him, my mother and the rest of the kids, and Nick and I soon followed.

And today, almost 35 years later, part of our family returned to the launching pad if you wish, to the city where it all began. To the initial Home. It feels funny to say this, but it's right.

Here is where all began.

I reminisce and if I close my eyes, I can relive all those wonderful moments, spent with so many of our friends, like the Baraks and the Feldioreanus and the Selageas.

It is good to be in a house of mourning the Bible says, because it makes us realize how fleeting we are.

We have to surrender to God's plans even when we don't understand or we don't accept it—yet. Death is a reality we all have to face. Our lives are so vulnerable and full of weaknesses. We all have needs, and mostly we can handle them alone, but many we cannot handle, even if there are people around us.

One of the problems is sin. The second is death. God has a right to call back his own, but how do we handle death? In 1Thessalonians 4:14-16, Paul explains that he wants you to know what happens, because knowledge gives you stability. Those who die in Christ, are going to a holding place, and one day they will rise again.

And sitting in church and taking it all in, the flowers, the people and the service, my face full of tears, I whisper: Here is where it all began. And here it is also, where will end, for some of us.

For Claudius (our cousin), the life story ended here.

Where will mine end, I do not know. It began here, and I have the reassurance that it will end ... in heaven....

Preparing to Leave on Vacation

I don't even know where to start. Well, I will start here. For the past month I have been traveling and have been to three states. Started with Oregon, then back to California, then Georgia, then back home. And today I am on a flight to Florida. How did this happen? I really do not know. It is God and only Him.

To think that only six months ago I was not even able to walk into a grocery store without being raked with anxiety. And now I am traveling by myself, which is strictly nothing short of a miracle. In fact, my life has been one miracle after another since He has called me forth.

So, last night I was home preparing to leave—laundry, cleaning, packing. I have arranged for the dogs to go to my parents because they love spending time with them. When I told Adrianne earlier via a very short conversation, she was not pleased. They are our dogs, Mom, and you need to ask us too, to which I replied, "Yes they are, but I am and have been their caretaker, so I did not feel it was necessary to ask. Plus, our family is so divided, so I am not sure how to even address and continue to be in a relationship with any of you."

"Have you told Caleb?" she asked.

"No, "but I will." That was the end.

In the kitchen just a few hours later, I informed him of my decision. I expected him to not be happy—to have something to say. After all, this is Caleb, the young man who can debate a dead person to life, if you know what I mean. But he took this to such a different level that, as I write my thoughts down, as I am flying to West Palm Beach, I am still flabbergasted, still in shock, still reeling. I tried to tell him that the decision had been made and to end the conversation, but he was not having it. I put my headphones on and while listening to music, I continued my work.

Not too long after that, he said, "I have made the decision to have Zoe stay here. She is not your dog. She in fact belongs to Barb and Rich, the old couple who lived in our care home."

"Even if that is true," I said, "I have been caring for them (Hazel was in the mix as well), and I believe it is better to have them cared for by your grandparents."

I am trying to gather the mental fortitude to describe what happened next, because he started to threaten to take the dogs so I wouldn't even have the chance to take them in the morning. I made the immediate decision to remove them from the kitchen and to maybe try to take them to my parents' house that night. I picked them both up and started to walk to my room and he was following me.

I said, "Caleb, please do not come into the room. This is my sanctuary and I do not want you to come in," but he did not comply. He came in with his arguments and his demeanor followed him. I then told him again to stop because if he didn't, I could also get the police involved, and then he challenged me.

"Do it," he said. "I dare you."

"Do not make me because if I have to, I will." I was trying to catch my breath. Still short of breath, I said while sobbing, "Lord, please help me." I also started to pray for wisdom, for peace in the midst of this, yet another storm. I knew he was capable of simply taking the dogs and not batting an eye, so I took them into my car with the idea of driving them to Martinez that night. And lo and behold, he followed me to the car, always threatening, and in effect, not allowing me to drive. He positioned himself inside the open door and said, "You are not going anywhere."

I reminded him that I could get the police and that he cannot do this, to which he again said," Do it!" At that point, I decided to dial 911.

"Emergency?"

"Yes," I said. "My name is DO and I am kindly asking for a police officer to come and settle a dispute between me and my son."

Many questions followed—many. And as the officers arrived, one stayed with me outside and one went inside with Caleb. I had run into both of them at the art and wine festival so I said hello and explained the situation: Divorce in process, emotions high, camps formed, need to clean, move out, sell and figure life out. He understood. Of course, as we were talking, Nick showed up because he was summoned by my son.

We all walked into the house where Caleb had talked to the second officer. He, (the officer) then proceeded to ask me very direct and stark questions.

"Mam, is the dog yours?"

"No," I explained. "But I am her caregiver."

"Mam, did you purchase the dog?"

"No, I said," but I am trying to adopt her."

"Mam, because you did not purchase the dog, you cannot take her."

"Yes," came a victorious gasp from Caleb. "Yes," he said again.

Can I please explain, officer," I asked him. By this time, both Nick and Caleb were jubilant. They thought they had their victory, but, not so fast.

As I was allowed to explain, all people present realized one thing quickly: Caleb had presented the situation very wrongly.

"You mean," the officer said, "that you are not leaving to go out of town with the dogs?"

"No sir," I said. "The dogs are going to be staying with my parents in Martinez."

"I am so sorry," came his apology. "I thought that you were . . . "

Yes of course you did, because when Caleb was at the car with me and heard me talk to the operator, he screamed, "My mom is committing theft and she has assaulted me."

What? Where did these words come from? What?

"Yes," he continued, "and she hit me, and this is a felony."

"Okay, you have not committed any crimes," the officer said, and I know that this is what he told the other officer when he talked to him in private. The officer's apology deflated Caleb's ego all of a sudden.

"My mom hit me and I have this on video," he said.

"The video is not important," the officer replied.

"Sir," I continued, "I did not hit my son. I did hit, if you wish, his phone when he was taking a video of me at the car, and I told him to please stop filming."

The officer in command said, "Okay, here is how we are going to solve this. First, Caleb, you stay out of it. This is between your parents."

Nick had his hand up, asking for his time. "Granted," said the officer.

He told them how we manage this business together and how things were handled, that we split our time of management there. I don't know how many days he said, but I said nine days and starting tomorrow he would be taking over the care home and that he was more than happy to watch Zoe.

In fact, like Caleb who was singing his own tune, he re-iterated how important it was for Zoe to be at the care home. Thinking back as I write, I now realize the "fight" was for Zoe only. Hazel was not really mentioned. Poor baby girl. You, too, are very, very important to me, and I hope that you will be going to Babi's house while Mom is gone.

The proposal from the officers was that we, Nick and my-self, will have to agree and compromise. I told him I do not agree. I asked him to please make a decision for us and we will follow it, and everyone agreed.

"So," he said. "Let the owner decide."

Okay, I like that. I will ask LisAnne in the morning, and then they left. I will not describe here the words and horrific insults that came out of my son's mouth afterwards. I will sim-ply say that they will remain forever etched in my memory.

Early in the morning I sent the text. Asked permission, filled her in as to Zoe's medical status, how she was just seen by the vet and still has infected ears, and that her stomach was upset and she was still vomiting every single day, and explained the bloodwork results. And again, I asked permis-sion for her to be in the care of my parents until I return. And the answer came quickly: "Yes, I am okay with this. Have a nice trip."

Lord, you are so good! You showed up again, and this time you served justice. Because Caleb's whole "war" had nothing to do with the fact that Zoe would be going to my parents, but more to do with the fact that he was not consulted, that I did not include him or the other two in the decision I had made, and he wanted to teach me a lesson. Well sadly, nobody won this war. Though Zoe is with the best caregivers, the heart of a mother broke again . . . sank in the deep pit again . . . hearing the accusation of her beloved son, echoed of course by my beautiful daughter and without doubt by the one who was supposed to love me until death do us part.

Lord, you allowed this to happen for a reason. Did I overreact? Was I too quick to call? Should I have allowed him to take the dogs and again bow my head to the demands of my son? Lord? And His answer came quickly: You have acted appropriately. Do not let anyone put more burdens on you. You have carried more than enough. You will walk this road without them, because they have hardened their hearts. And I, the Lord, will carry you. Hold on to me and hang tight. It will get worse, but the victory has been won. I will take you to green pastures and still waters (Psalm 23).

Lord, and this Florida trip was planned by you, right?

Just go and feel, breathe, relax, sing, dance, rest, eat, laugh, and tell that beautiful cousin Shy that I have her as well in the palm of my hand.

I sure will, Lord. I sure will!

Do Not Pass Me By

I have been in Georgia for four days now. Four! I came here very apprehensive. Never been or was interested in learning more about this state. It's the South. Need I need say more? I read about it in books, history books that is, about slavery—yes that dirty "S" word, that happened in the South. *Uncle Tom's Cabin* was a book that marked me for years. The movie Roots, which we watched back in my native county with subtitles because my use and knowledge of the English language was so limited at that time, affected me as well. So, the South for me brought to mind these kinds of emotions.

Of course, today we are in 2022, and the joy of seeing my sister, who had just moved here a big whopping month ago, had sent me into excitement. I knew about the Georgia Peach. I knew about it being a red state and now from what I was told, it was changing into a blue state. I listened to Michael Bubble's rendition of "Georgia on My Mind' way too many times. And that's about all!

But today, as I pen my meditation down, I am fully convinced that I will leave part of my heart here. Trying to write things down so I won't forget a moment of my trip here, as if to say that every single day, hour, minute, and second that passed, had meaning. And these moments carefully crafted by the Creator Himself, these stories, will live in me for a long, long time.

I will jump to the unfolding of todays, knowing that all the days will be painted before the ink of this page is dry. Because we are in the month of Elul and because of my amazing friend Dori, who reconnected me to our (and I say this because all of us followers of Christ have been grafted into Israel) Jewish roots, I have decided to accept the King's invitation and meet with Him in the fields—quite literally.

Out by a magnificent tree, reminding me of the Tree at Mamre, this morning I met with the Lord. My vocabulary is poor to try to describe the overflow of His presence! Because when His beloved accepts His invitation, He manifests in ways unimaginable. I sang, I read, I prayed, I cried, I repented, I surrendered, I shouted for joy, I praised, I listened, I bowed, I fell prostrate, I stood up, I danced, I lifted my body, heart, and spirit to the one who knows my name—called me out of prison, loved me from the beginning of time, wrote my name in His book of life, and who considered me worthy to be spoiled over this long Labor Day weekend and nudged me to come.

Because from the eternity passed, He orchestrated this meeting at the Leleus family Mamre tree.

A meeting where He bestowed on me so many gifts of His Holy Spirit that as I write this last paragraph, my heart is so full I cannot find any more eloquent words to say other than, "My Lord, if now I have favor in your sight, please do not pass by your servant without stopping to visit. Genesis 18:3-4

Sola Scriptura! Solo Christo! Sola Fide! Soli Deo Gloria!!!

EXTENDED GRACE
AND PERSONAL BELIEFS

Meet Chris Lilies

Can I tell you a story? Thank you for being kind and listening to my heart. Tonight as I was driving home from Mom's (I went there because I wanted her to try the lymphedema pump), I started to not feel well. It was sudden; chills, body aches. Hmmmm. What is this? Covid! No Lord, not now. Not for me, but for the ones that I could have exposed. Nelutu is positive and Emi was there at the party on Sunday and then came to Ben's. My mind reeled. I need to get tested. Oh God, please not now . . .

I got home and realized that I didn't have any tests so off to CVS in Walnut Creek, I went. Going downstairs to tell Caleb, he was on the phone. "Could I please talk to you for a minute?

"Mom, I'm busy. Give me five."

I said, "Please, I need to talk to you *now*," and reluctantly he got off the phone.

"Caleb, I might have been exposed to Covid and I don't feel good."

"Stay away from me," he yelled, covering his nose.

I said, "I'm at the foot of the bed I don't think you need to worry." He got even more upset and had to leave the room.

Back from CVS where I brought a thermometer and a test, I had no fever and the rest, well . . . something went wrong. Call customer service a thought came and I got mad, and I did. You think anyone answers at 1 a.m.? So back to CVS I went. I exchanged the faulty test with a new one and said, "Could I please stay here until it develops? I don't want to go home and come back."

The lady at the checkout was quite nice and said, "Of course."

"Where can I sit so I don't bother anyone?" I asked. Not that there were any people at CVS at that hour but behind the counters there were chairs in front of the photo printing stations, so she invited me to sit there.

"Perfect," I said. "I will go sit there. Thank you."

As I sat down and started my nose swabbing yet again, I noticed a black man sitting two chairs down.

He looked homeless. As the timer was counting down fifteen minutes, I went to the car to get my sweet dog Hazel, and for the next almost thirty minutes, I was immersed into the life of Chris. Forty-five years old, born in San Francisco. Lived in Oakland. Never knew his father. His mother did her best but the neighborhood was rough.

"Are you on drugs?" I asked?

He nodded. "Meth."

I said, "You have any on you? Can I see?" He showed me how he smokes it.

"Expensive?"

"If you want pure, yeah, because they mix all kind of junk in it otherwise."

Oh Lord, I can't take this image. Homeless for nine years, sleeps in the elevator at the Cheesecake Factory because it's warm. Not supposed to, but security is nice and wakes him up before the day comes. Was in the park for three years and in and out of shelters. As he was answering my questions,

I felt him to be kind. He smiled. He was respectful. Had not washed in years but for some reason he did not smell (I also had cold-like symptoms and most likely could not smell normally).

"If I give you money tonight, what would you use it for?" I asked him.

"I'd like to get a room at Motel 6," he replied

"Do they rent to people without homes?" I inquired.

"Yes and no," he told me.

Oh God, my heart is heavy. He was fiddling with an old phone.

"You got one?" I asked.

"Just bought it from a friend. Ten dollars with a card," he answered.

"You got a number?" I asked him.

"I think so," he told me, and I wrote it down.

"Do you need clothes?"

"I have some on my bike."

"You do?"

"Yeah. Well, I have one pair of long pants that ripped so I have these shorts and this thick jacket," he replied with a smile that showed two missing front teeth.

"Are you hungry? Can I get you anything?"

"No, I had a salad, but I'm thirsty."

"Whatever you want," I told him.

He said, "I need some electrolytes."

I wanted to break down and cry. I said, "Chris do you know that God loves you?"

"Yeah," he said. "I have a Bible."

"You do? Can I see it?" He pulled out a Gideon New Testament. "Oh, I'm so happy, Chris, God really loves you and wants to rock your world tonight." He picked up a lemonade and some mustard pretzels.

Oh Lord, such sweetness in such a rough lived life. I got him some chocolate and gum and gave him $100. "Please don't use it on meth," I said.

"I'm not," he said, though I'm not sure he can resist.

"Walk with me to my car. I have some cookies there I want you to have," I said.

He was so thankful, and as I gave him a hug, I made a promise to myself that I will pray for him. And as I was driving home, I got madder than hell—mad at this unfair world and at the life he lived. No support—got in a lot of trouble. How can he not? And he told me he has a son in Stockton. My heart bleeds for that boy who was denied the presence of a dad in his life because of these horrible life circumstances.

I got home and could not sleep. I cleaned my kitchen like I've not done in a while. I was too hurt, angry, and mad at this world. "I won't sleep tonight," I told myself. "I simply can't." But then I remembered, I too need rest like my friend Chris. So as I laid myself down to sleep, talking to the Lord, I said, "Use me for your glory, Lord. Make me whole again and use me, Lord."

Good night world. Tonight God took care of this man and in God's perfect timing he orchestrated this. And for this, I am grateful.

Pushed Up Against the Wall

I don't think I ever thought I would live a time when in society, and in the family, all my convictions and morals, and actually my whole being, would be pushed up against the wall. Against *their* wall. Against everything I was raised to believe and I adopted as my own philosophy for life. But yes, I am living this time, and I would venture to say that it is both challenging and hard. No . . . who am I kidding? It's actually horrendously difficult but also excitingly good.

They say, or, rather, it is said, that fire refines gold. They say, or rather, it is said, that when the rubber meets the road, it is when one can show who he or she truly is. So as I ponder, and as I try to formulate an answer to all these questions coming my way, I can start by saying this: It is amazing to be alive when history writes its last pages—by all intent and purposes, and by looking around to all that is happening. But most importantly, by studying eschatology, the end of times events described in the Holy Scriptures, one can deduce with certainty that we are the last generation.

Why do I describe this as exciting? Well, because by the way we live, by the way we act, and by the way we talk, we can contribute, rush, and aid the Lord Jesus Christ's return. The end of Revelation, the last book of the Bible, states: "Amen come Lord Jesus! Blessed is he who awaits His return." Revelation 22:17. We are told clearly what is going to happen and how we should live. Pretty clear instructions, pretty black and white, yet not always easy to follow and implement.

The Scripture says: There will be wars and rumors of wars . . . famine . . . epidemics . . . People will be haters of truth, exchanging the truth for a lie, creating their own reality, denying God, aligning with the evil that says: You were born this way, after all love is what matters, who are they hurting? Why can't we marry whomever we want and love? Gay marriage was legalized a long time ago, because we are now talking about transgender issues—issues of minors, changing the age of consent, reinstating abortion, letting each state decide because the general consent is: My body, my right to choose, without realizing that they're hurting the very core of society—the family, as God intended it to be.

Am I describing something familiar? Is anyone with me? Is anyone as horrified as I am to see and know that so many children are disrespectful of their parents and of any organ of power and order? The Bible says clearly that in the last days, children will turn against parents and parents against children—a horrible reality of the times we live in today. Yes, indeed. Yes, indeed.

I decided today, November 8, 2022, that I will not cast my vote. I came to America as a young adult looking for freedom of speech manifested among other things in the right to vote which I exercised for many years, except today. I know this might upset some people, and I am sorry. But I know deep in my heart that my vote will not affect one iota of what is about to happen. I simply don't feel that if I had voted, a dent would have been placed in any of the amendments.

My state always wins as a democratic liberal state. Plain and simple. And I could hear comments from people who would say: "Move." But It is not that simple. It's a huge state on the West Coast of this beautiful United States of America but none the less, it is full of hatred and lack of tolerance for people who vote differently than the majority, for people who believe differently than the majority, and for people who live with different perspectives and morals in mind.

Yes, tonight as I'm trying to put my thoughts down in my journal, I can say for sure that I've been pushed to the limit. My hand has been twisted in an attempt to accept an agenda that goes against everything that I am. But I can say with confidence that I will stand for the truth, which is only found in the word of God. I will stand against the breaking of the marriage that is so prevalently encouraged and accepted. And I will stand against any measures that detest God's principles, commandments, and laws.

I came to America for freedom, but today I feel that my freedom is being taken away—first in my own home, and then in society. But, prompted by the Holy Spirit and hearing the whisper of my sweet Jesus, I press on, persevering and desiring to stand firm, and uncompromising until the end, when I will bow in front of Him, beholding His glorious face, to hear the words that I so wish and desire to hear: Come good and faithful servant and inherit what was prepared for you, and falling at His feet, I will worship Him and cast down my crown.

And I wish again to hear Him say: "Well done, my daughter. Well Done."

I Don't Want to Be So Easily Bothered

It's not easy for me to write about this because it's exposing me as a person who gets easily frustrated. It's not always the case, but lately I have struggled to not let all that I am going through get to me. It seemed to always be, and the scenario repeated itself many times like this: Nothing worked well and together! Let me say it again—nothing worked well and together!

Can anybody identify with me?

I was living each day stumbling upon every little thing, as if all of it was just a big bunch of hurdles, hurdles that I couldn't get past and jump over. And the frustration built up and spilled over into not so beautiful music.

Let me give you some examples: You are in a hurry to get somewhere on time and all—and I mean all the stoplights are red—all. Coincidence, happenstance, or just the Holy Spirit trying to use these moments to teach and to admonish. You try to finish a task, and just when you're about done, something falls to the ground and makes a mess. You're unable to open something that is needed to complete the task and you are forced to leave it undone. You come out of an appointment and you see that you got a parking ticket just because you were two minutes late. Oh, this one doesn't sit well with me at all.

By the way, who likes to have this kind of job—to check on meters and if someone missed one or two minutes past the time limit you write them tickets. Who enjoys having a job like this?

I would not make a good ticket giver because I would put money into their meters, just enough so then they would not run over the time limit.

Lately I've been pondering about God, and about the fact that He is light, and darkness cannot overpower him! There's nothing darkness can do when light walks into a room. No, there is not!

And if I make a conscious decision to live in the light, nothing and no one will bother me again. No. It. Won't!

Demi the Diva

When I was asked by a good friend of mine if I would be willing to volunteer some of my time to help in a foster care program, I immediately said yes. I didn't know anything about this program, but I wanted to be part of volunteering through a church. This was not at my church, but it didn't matter. The three of us were going to go—me, her, and her mother, to watch children while their parents attended class. "Okay, I can do this," I told myself, looking forward to it.

We arrived at the church after circling around the neighborhood about five times because the GPS was confused, which made us laugh and feel frustrated at the same time. Not to compare us to the people of Israel, who circled around the promised land for forty years, but we too circled around the church, trying to stay calm.

None of us knew what to expect. We met with the organizers who gave us instructions about what we had to do, and we were very excited to see the children come in. We greeted them and made name tags for them, not feeling quite prepared for what might lay head. It had been many years since I was surrounded by so many children. My job and my passion had put me around elderly people, so this was unchartered territory. We placed some of the name tags on their backs so they would not lose them or take them off while playing.

One by one, the kids came in, most of them wearing big grins on their little faces. White, Black and Asian, these were children living in foster homes. As I looked at them, my heart hurt knowing that their own parents had either abandoned them or were not in any position to provide for them. And at that moment my heart also warmed for these parents, who had taken it upon themselves to provide love and care for these beautiful children. Many were normal kids, but some had handicaps which were very obvious.

We had two hours with them and besides us, there were two more ladies serving with us. Okay, what should I do?

I felt a little strange because I was so out of practice. My heart wrapped around this little girl who was wearing corrective eyeglasses, and who had a smile as big as her face. I asked her, "Do you like to dance?" She gave a me funny look. Okay, maybe at her young age she had never been exposed to dancing, so I said, "How about we play some music and you and I can walk around like divas?"

"Divas?" she asked. "What's a diva?"

"Okay, let me show you," I replied, and we strutted up and down the room to the tune of some kind of music playing on a small, portable CD player. I looked at her face and saw how much she was enjoying it. "Work it—hold your head up tall, walk like a diva," I told her. "Come on, work it!"

Catching on fast, one of boys in the room walked over and asked if he could join us. "Of course," I said. "Show us your best walk!" And like a runway model, he did such a perfect strut, flipping his hair and trying to swivel his hips. Catwalk worthy indeed I was thinking as the tears started to form in my eyes. Such innocence!

Unaware maybe of their grim circumstances, mingling with strangers, these children allowed themselves to have fun. One older boy came over to me and asked, "May I add something to your name tag?"

"Of course," I said. "Go ahead! And next to my name he wrote: "Demi, the diva!"

My eyes were full of tears—tears of joy of course, but also of sorrow because Jesus loved children. In one picture we have Him sitting with them on His lap and saying, "If you don't live like some of them, you will surely not enter the kingdom of God."

What does it mean to live like children? After all, we are

grown-ups. We surely can't live like them—the sweet children in front of me right now. Like them? And I've heard the Holy Spirit whisper, "Yes, like them! Be innocent like them. Be sweet like them. Be trusting like them. Be inquisitive like them. Be full of joy like them. Be . . . in your heart . . . just like a child . . . it's a requirement for entering the kingdom."

Augh! So like you, Lord, to use every moment to teach me, to admonish me, to touch me ever so tenderly. Like a good Father! Yes, You are!

Leaving the church after the program finished, my name tag was given a very important place in my car—on the dashboard. Laughing back at me, the words seem to remind me. Demi the Diva, huh? Just don't forget! My beautiful T and your mama, I can't wait to go back again. I'm sure you feel the same way too! Until next time sweet children . . . until next time.

Two Days Ago, My Life was Shaken When My Daughter Walked Into My Home

It had been ten months since I'd seen her, and on a whim a few days before, I sent her a text. I was curious to see if she had unblocked me, but my text was delivered. "Wow," I thought. There is progress." I told myself that she would probably not answer but to my surprise, she did.

"How are you doing," I asked her.

"I am not well," she replied. "I want to die, and suicide is on my mind."

My heart quickened! No . . . but yes . . . of course you are. What do you expect? Lord have mercy, Lord, intervene. No, but yes, and on and on, and round and round I went. Lord . . . am I ready for this? And what should I do? You have pulled me out of this pit. I too, was there—I know the pain. I felt Him telling me: "Reach out," and I did, and the next day she parked her car in front of my house and, walked in.

I thought I was going to cry, but I did not. She looked lost . . . incredibly out of touch with reality. She surveyed my home and said, "This is so strange. This feels weird. Your house is so nice. How can you afford this place?" to which I said, "God provides, Adrianne." I invited her to have dinner with me (it was eight o'clock in the evening). She looked messy, unkept, so I started to ask questions.

"How are things at home?"

"Fine," she said.

"Well, if they are fine, why are you so disheveled?" I thought about asking, but then I stopped. I did not want to sound critical. I've been hit when I was down, and it does not feel good. Slowly she opened-up. She had lost the desire to live. She messed up all her relationships. She could not function at work. She slept in an unmade bed for weeks. She has no clean clothes.

I silently prayed, "Lord, what should I say?" I'm not surprised, but no, I can't go down this road. She is hurting enough. So I shared my testimony. I told her how God called me out of the grave, and I ran. I told her that He was my *hiding place*, my *safe place*, my *rock*, my *helper*. I told her that He is leading me every day and I joyfully follow. And then I brought it home for her and said, "He is the *only one* who can heal your broken soul, Adrianne."

She listened and then said, "This Christian thing is not for me. I've tried it and it does not work."

Oh, how I hurt for her in that moment. Because she

believed the lies of the enemy who had convinced her that God is not real if she can't see Him and understand with logic. So, she decided this is not for her. I knew at that moment that the battle was fierce, for my daughter was raised to know the truth of the gospel. She recited the Psalms, and she sang in the youth group. And though I know those don't give salvation, the seeds had been planted. But at some point in her life, when she was in college, she decided to venture out and seek for herself. Mom's faith was restrictive and she wanted freedom.

And freedom she found, or so she thought. Because today sitting on my couch was a very broken woman shackled by her life's poor choices and failures. Holy Spirit . . . only You can transform her. Only You can heal her. Lord Jesus, your blood was shed for my daughter as well, and all her sins will be washed clean, if . . . she . . . confesses. Well, she is far from that contrition. She has yet to surrender.

So, later in the night after she showered and fell asleep in my nice clean bed in the guest room, her mama went to war against the enemy of her daughter's soul—declaring that this house is holy ground, telling him that he is trespassing, asking him to leave, in the powerful name of the risen Christ! This house is the Lord's.

His light shines in the darkness and since I know he hates the light I told him he has no business being here. I claimed my ground. I covered it in the precious blood of Jesus and exhausted, I fell asleep praying: Lord, you got this. Lord, you brought me here for such a time as this. Lord, you have a plan. Use me, clean me, fill me so I can be at your service.

I don't know what tomorrow will bring but I will trust in you. And for now, I'm just glad she is sleeping peacefully here.

Like Birds Perched Up on a Pole

I don't know about you, but many times when I drive, I look up to the sky and on many poles on the freeway or on the streets, I see birds. Many birds in fact, sitting one next to the other. At times, I counted ten. And I often wondered what exactly are they doing up there, kind of huddled together, one next to the other up on top of the pole.

Even today as I'm driving to church for the Christmas Eve service, on the freeway, there are many light poles on each side of the road. And I noticed the birds, way on top, and wondered if they were watching the freeway, the traffic, the cars, and wondering if they worry about falling. But then I correct myself, saying, "They are birds. At any moment they can fly away. They don't just fall off a pole if they have healthy wings that is, and if they, the birds, are not sick.

Because I like analogies, my mind goes to us, the human race. In the Scriptures we read: "Do not worry about anything if God takes care of the flowers in the fields and of the birds in the air, how much more will He care for you, oh you of little faith?" Jesus says at some point. See Matthew 6:25-33. And He was right, because He knew that our propensity would be to worry, to be afraid of falling, to be afraid of stumbling, to be afraid of not being able to get up.

And boy did I experience that. For many years, fear was my constant companion. Most of my fears were unfounded—fear of going into a store, fear of being judged by people, fear of being seen in public and judged, fear of not being able to function, fear of talking in public. Yes, me. Because for many, many, years, I had no problems—singing at weddings, reciting poems in front of the church, singing solos, being in front of people, conducting meetings, teaching classes, giving concerts, managing a business.

But now I was afraid of my own shadow. How? What happened to me that I was so afraid? And the answer is worth noting: I walked away. I walked off from under the umbrella of God. I tried to manage my life, asking God for wisdom, asking him to answer my prayers, but expecting, almost demanding, that He will say yes to all my needs.

Idolatry was the sin that I was guilty of. I put my marriage and definitely my husband on the pedestal of my heart. I fought for him for five long and hard years — one would say that I did that all my life, and it would not be wrong, thinking that this is God's will, expecting God to answer, and desiring Him to restore my marriage and my family.

But today, I'm driving to church alone, with my family far from away from me, both my children estranged from me, and of course my husband, a stranger himself, actually walking on the road to a final divorce. Yes, the ugly "D" word for me is divorce.

One can ask, "Why, Lord? Why have we gotten here? How come You, Lord, didn't answer my prayers? I was told a million times that God hates divorce and I know the verse quite well. So again, one begs the question: Why? Why not? Why not?

But the answer remains: Yes, He is able. But in His sovereign plan for me today, He has me walk a different road — a road of obedience, a road of submission, and a road where He leads, and I follow. I am following, totally loving Him, because He is still the only one who doesn't disappoint. He is the one who takes the fear away as we were told in the book of Isaiah: "Fear not, for I am with you. I have called you by name, child, you are Mine. When you walk through the valley, I will be there, through the waters you will not drown and the fires will not burn you".

And like the birds perched up on street poles, I can confidently say: He is my protector, He's my redeemer, He is my savior. Praise God. Glory Hallelujah. He has come, Immanuel, with us. Merry Christmas everyone!

Follow Peace with All Men, and Holiness, without Which No Man Shall See the Lord. (Hebrews 12 :14)

Reading from my morning devotional, I came across this question: "Do you have a difficult relationship in your life, poisoned by offense, bitterness or misunderstanding?" (Oh boy, do I!) "It doesn't matter who it is; it could be your spouse, your sibling, your child, your parent, your friend, and so on. The Scripture clearly tells us to follow peace with all men. That includes the list above!"

Because the author is a Greek scholar, he gives new emphasis on the word "follow." In Greek, the world is *diakos*, and it refers to an old hunting term that meant to follow the tracks of an animal, the scent of an animal, and to look and search for that animal until you finally get your prey. Remember, this refers to a hunter (thus the idea of a wounded animal is described here).

The idea, I guess, is that when you have to follow peace, you are to search for it until you find it. You are not to stop until you reach that goal—to track it down because peace doesn't just come to us. So we have to do something to find peace with people, no matter how difficult a particular relationship is, God is telling us that it is our responsibility to try to mend it.

Though we are *not* responsible for what the other person does, we *are* responsible for what we do! Of course, sometimes we do everything we can, but the person doesn't respond. We cannot answer for the other person's attitude, but we are going to have to answer for ourselves.

I struggle and have been struggling to find peace over what happened in my life, especially in the past year or so. So many things that I never thought I would go through. Divorce brought so much craziness. I never would've dreamed in a million years that something this crazy would happen to me. To us. Never! Nothing prepared me for it! But it seems that God is trying to catch my attention this morning, saying: "Follow the tracks of peace," because the Bible goes on to tell us that the reason we are to follow peace with all men is that, "Without it no man shall see the Lord." Hebrews 12:14b.

The world sees and tells us that "lack of peace serves as a blocker and stops us from experiencing the presence of God. And it goes even deeper to say that we are to follow "after holiness," and that we are called to a higher standard. But we cannot do it without the presence of the Holy Spirit living in us and giving us the power to walk in forgiveness.

We are called to walk in holiness. We are called to follow after peace. We are called to walk free from offense. Otherwise, we will remain in a life filled with strife and bitterness, and we won't be really able to experience the tangible presence of God. All good. All understood in my mind. But there's a long road for this to travel from my head to my heart. Yes, there is.

Like my friend Cindy used to say: "Sanctification

happens in small bites." As long as we move forward, one small step at a time, victory is ours guaranteed through Him, and only through Him. Putting boots on the ground rather than just living in a theologically sound and filled with knowledge life is what living a Christian life at this time in history means.

I pray that the Holy Spirit will lead me and show me what path to take in this pursuit so I can please the Lord by walking filled with the Holy Spirit. That is the desire of my heart and my prayer I lift to the throne of grace this morning. I will end with a poem I wrote years ago called "Holiness."

I read in Your word that I am holy,
Sanctified, put aside, a special vessel indeed.
Why is this so hard to believe, oh Father?
Is it because I live every day,
Surrounded by sin?

Surely not by deeds, but by faith,
I can fathom,
The holiness that You bestow upon me.
They then, do I listen to the enemy's voices:
You are holy?
Pot of clay, look at you!
Can't you see?

Holy is God, we all know that,
And tremble!
But you?
Look again!
You're just making me laugh!

Enough!
I will not listen to your lies any longer!
He says I am holy!
I am!
So, just stop!

He says if I stay in His word,
If I listen,
His holiness will reflect upon me,
Like a mirror reflects the image of a vessel,
Standing face to face with it,
Perfectly!

I want to live my life out, in victory.
I am holy!
Oh, Father, please help me believe!
Through and through, sanctified,
Put aside and devoted,
To be used by You, dear God,
Exclusively!

Empower me daily,
To live and be ready,
To share this with all who will listen,
Because You say, I am holy because YOU are holy!
Oh, vessel of clay,
Believe and rejoice!

Written After I attended Anna's Funeral

For reasons maybe known or not, here it is. In the still of the night when darkness engulfs me, I turn on a very dim light with a golden bulb and arrange my pillows around me. I breathe deep and exhale slowly. My mind is trying not to go back to the images that so deeply affected me today— two beautiful, young, vibrant girls, honoring the memory of their equally beautiful mother, now gone.

The youngest, Bianca, had to be given a raiser to reach the mic because she is still so young, just eleven years old. She wrapped herself in her mother's favorite sweater and a red scarf adorned her supple neck. Her mother's as well, I am sure. With the voice of such innocence, chocked by abundant tears, she shared. And in my own space, somewhere in the middle of this magnificent cathedral, I sat transfixed, my soul worshipping the Lord who at this very moment had Anna in His presence.

Overwhelmed by grief, I whispered, "Lord, you do not ever make mistakes. Nothing takes you by surprise. In fact, You are in total control." My mind reeled. Lord . . . how about me, Lord? How do I walk this road that seems so heavy for me right now? Lord, You know, You see. You are the only one who loves me unconditionally.

Lord, there are so many facts that are wrong and so many against me, waiting it seems, for me to make a mistake so they can pounce, ready to hurt, to accuse, to super analyze. I have been called such horrific epithets by the one who was supposed to be my protector, my best friend and husband. I am reprimanded and corrected more frequently than not, by my beautiful girl. Lord, how do I navigate this? How do

I stand knowing that in order to survive, I have to walk this road?

The memorial service for this beautiful woman of God was one of the most beautiful services I have ever attended, and I have attended many. From the music to the speeches, to the majesty of the cathedral, to the white balloons released from the steps of the church. It was a sunny day, and the image of the balloons flying up into the skies will be forever etched in my mind.

So many questions overflow my heart. How will these beautiful and innocent souls, traverse life without their mama? Who will comfort the husband who carried his wife's casket, and who's tears were flowing freely? Who will soothe the pain of her parents, her sister's and loved ones?

What happens to all their dreams that were cut so short, it seems by this unforgiving diagnosis?

And why is it, that people tell how magnificent one is, only at their funeral?

Must we wait until then, to tell one how much they mean to us?

And bringing it, into my perspective, I surrender myself again to Him who knows and sees.

My family (husband and children) not by my side, I again close my eyes, and at the sound of the church bells, I say:

I will, for the first time in my life, walk with You alone, make decisions with You alone, travel and trust in You alone, and entrust me into Your loving arms, where all pain for a moment subsides, and in the presence of the divine, I trust and wait.

And the Word Became Flesh
and Dwelt Among Us

In a manger, in the town of Bethlehem, the cries of a new-born baby filled the air. Two young parents welcomed their firstborn into the world. But He was no ordinary newborn because the world was created by Him. He was the Word, who like John says in his first chapter was with God, and the Word was God. It almost sounds like a play on words but if you read carefully, the first few verses of the Gospel of John all make sense. The Word was Jesus and Jesus was with God, and Jesus was God.

Having almost finished Bible study about the Trinity, this really jumps out everywhere from the pages of the Scripture. Trying to imagine the Creator in the form of a newborn baby makes for a good movie for Christmas, some beautiful songs, Christmas carols, and cards.

How many pictures have been painted through the centuries depicting baby Jesus? Surrounded by animals in swaddling clothes, some even pictured Him shivering because of His environment! Laying in hay! I don't know that any of this was true, and I don't think it's that important. More important is that the divine came down in the body of a newborn baby. Took on flesh and yes in the beginning, beautiful flesh—baby flesh.

I don't know why I'm so hung up on this, this morning. This imagery is not leaving my mind. And other than the shepherds visiting and later the Maggi, not much was given in the Bible about the life of Jesus as a baby, as a young child, if you wish, the son of God, the son of David, the son of Joseph the Son of Mary. We see them fleeing to Egypt to escape the wrath of Herod. We see Jesus in the temple at age twelve, engaging with the priests and the people there. And then, we see Him starting his public ministry when He was thirty years old. Everything else is left to our human imagination as far as his early life was concerned.

I know many wonder just like I do, what was Jesus like growing up? What was He like as a young boy? A teenager? A young adult? What did He do? How did He live His life? How did He relate to his parents? His siblings? His relatives?

Many were wondering when they saw Him perform miracles, asking, "Is He not the son of Josef the carpenter?" And if his father was a carpenter, did Jesus help him? Did the one who created the human body, take wood and fashion a beautiful piece of furniture? Carpentry deals with wood. I'm wondering what his father, earthly father that is, made out of wood.

And how did Jesus handle being a human and divine at the same time? The Bible says he was tempted just like us, but without sin. My mind goes to many places. There are so many questions I would ask the Lord if I had the chance to interview him. Did He obey his mother? Did He obey his father? How did He relate to his younger siblings? Did Jesus ever get sick? He who healed sickness and raised the dead . . . hmmmm.

I don't know about this, but we know the Bible is silent when it comes to this. No information given! Because it wasn't important? My inquiring mind wants to know. The Lord gave me a vivid memory and imagination.

It's Him. He poured it into me. I always say you cannot teach talent. And it's true. Just as true is one being anointed because it is not the work of men but of the Holy Spirit. Plain and simple and true. I know I'm speaking to someone today.

Jesus is truly the reason I'm alive today because darkness had engulfed me and the enemy of my soul wanted to destroy me. So I sing with all fervency. Nothing but the blood! Nothing but the blood! Nothing but the blood!

And today, I am content and want to be better. Not for me, but for the kingdom of God. I want to occupy until He comes back, like Amir Tsarfati always says. I borrowed the sentence from him.

Yes, I want to do KINGDOM work, like my good friend Dori says. While I wait for the divorce process to be finalized, and it looks like it is going to drag on for many more months to come. As per his wishes, I will wait, but not in vain. No, I will wait by being busy—spreading the gospel, helping the sick and the poor, blessing my church and its leaders. And also, I will plan to enjoy the ending of this year. A year of the favor of the Lord. A year of amazing favor.

Because He came down and walked the roads in Jerusalem and surrounding cities with one main purpose in mind—to save souls. And we are to follow suit. Will you join me?

The Junk Drawer of Our Hearts

Who does not have a junk drawer in their home? By the show of hands or head nods, I can see that everyone does—all of us have at least one. Today at Bible Study when that question was asked, someone said: "I have a junk room, a junk garage, and a few junk drawers." Regardless of what or how many, let's talk about the "junk" we store in our hearts. Boy, where should I start? I'm having trouble formatting a list.

Naturally, I would start with this: In my kitchen junk drawers, I usually throw in stuff that I don't want to deal with at that particular moment, always saying, "I'll deal with it later." But later never comes, or it only comes when the drawer is so full it doesn't close or open anymore.

If we must make this analogy regarding our hearts, I can maybe start by saying that what is inside of it is stuff that I didn't want or do not want to deal with, for many different reasons. Let's look inside and see what we find. Frustration greets me, but why? How come? Where did it start and how long have I stored it? First and foremost, many times frustration came from not understanding God nor His will for my life.

I consider myself a student of the word of God who is hungry for a deeper understanding of the Scriptures, so it comes only naturally to try to figure it out. Sounds very normal and is where many of us are, but it's not always easy and can be rather hard. So, I throw it in the drawer, mutter and complain, cover sniffles and tears, and move on . . . or so I think.

Unforgiveness is another big occupant in my drawer, and even though I testify many times that I have forgiven my trespassers, I seem to always return to the drawer to get another whiff of that scent which turns more putrid with time. On the same team with unforgiveness is anger, which spurs anxiety and depression of course, and when not dealt with properly, brings a desire for revenge, accompanied by self-pity and excuse making, and feelings of entitlement, especially when we have been hurt so deeply.

"I deserve to feel this way," I have told the Lord so many times. "You see the way I've been hurt, don't you, God?"

But the junk drawer does not always contain only personal emotions, but social emotions as well, related to the environment we live in, the political party which governs our country, and the geopolitical crisis that overwhelms humanity. Yeah, these too overload my junk drawer. There is a reason I do not watch the news, although much news comes in from my iPad, and I can't resist not opening it. Yuck, stop, I can't, it's not helping, need to know, why, God? Voices yelling, "If God is good why does He . . . ?" It's not Him but the sinful nature. Ears covered and eyes blinded by the culture. Counterculture weak. Stop, I can't erase it or take it.

In the drawer it goes and I slam it shut. Phew, it's over, for now. I will visit later. Almost makes us feel right to deposit all of this in our junk drawer, doesn't it? But sadly, when the drawer reopens, many times it explodes. Am I talking to someone? Am I touching some discord of our core values as human beings? I know I'm not alone in this, and I believe the sooner we try to clean our junk drawers, the better we will feel.

But a question that persists while I am cleaning is this: Do we clean the drawer only to have it filled up again? Or, do we take our cleaned junk drawer and fill it up with wholesome things? Do you know how to do this? Do I?

You are in good company, because Scripture says when we don't know we need to ask the Holy Spirit for wisdom. See James 1:5. If any of you lack wisdom, let him ask of God who gives . . ." 2 Corinthians 10:5. We take every thought captive to the obedience of Christ . . ."Matthew 7:7. "Seek and you shall find . . . ask and it will be given to you . . . knock and it will be opened," and so many other verses that have pretty much the same message: When fully surrendering our hearts, minds, and bodies to the power of the Holy Spirit, He comes and fills us to the fullest (though He also lives inside each believer in Jesus Christ).

And the power that resurrected Jesus Christ from death, cleanses our junk and makes our hearts anew. New hearts surrendered to God the Father, God the Son, and God the Holy Spirit are hearts so full, no room remains for any junk. Because its place has the field with new tenants. Glory Hallelujah!

Holding Worry Close . . . No More!

I don't know about you, but for a very long time now, I did not really obey the Scriptures that tell us: "Do not worry!" I mean, come on! How can we not worry about, this, that, or the other, especially when life hits us hard more often than not, most of the time through our loved ones?

And as women, I know I can get many Amens!

I have recited and memorized the passage from Philippians 4:4-8 my entire life, and it goes something like this: "Do not worry about anything, but in everything, by prayer and petition, with thanksgiving, make your request known to God. And the peace of God that transcends all understanding will guide your hearts and minds in Christ Jesus". And then Paul, the Apostle, proceeds to tell us what to focus on: "Whatever is true, whatever is noble, whatever is just and of good repute," he says. "Think about those things."

But have we? At times I know we did, but I speak for most of us when I say again (especially us women, mothers, and daughters), our tendency is to worry! Leaving Bible study this morning, my heart and spirit have been so fed in

the company of God and my God-seeking friends. Surrounded by the beautiful landscape at the farm (that's what
Cathy's house is called or known for), we dug into God's
word. We are studying the Trinity, and learning about each
of the three persons of our triune God: God the Father, God
the Son, and God the Holy Ghost. The study is deep.

It asks for time, discipline, and diligence, things that I
desperately need, especially at this time in my life. Because
the tendency is to bow to self-pity and find any excuse to
stay in self-loathing and self-victimization. So I have made
some changes and continue to keep myself accountable.

One of my new life resolutions, if you wish, was and is,
to dedicate more time to know my Creator God, my Savior,
Jesus Christ, and my Comforter, the Holy Spirit. And this
study did just that. As I read page after page, when I read
and do my daily assignment, and through group discus-
sions, I learn and discover so much.

So little of my time growing up in my church was dedi-
cated to teaching about the Holy Spirit. Sadly, so little. We
knew something about him—the Holy Spirit. We occasionally sang about Him, but to understand that He *is* the third
person of the trinity who lives in and all around us was a
concept I started to grasp only as I matured and got older.

But once I understood, once my eyes were open, I can
testify that I have no greater comfort than knowing that as
Jesus ascended to heaven, His promise of a Comforter came
true only about forty days later. And His assignment is to
minister, inhabit, comfort, teach, and intercede for us, and
this is just scratching the surface. What an amazing truth—
an amazing truth, indeed!

So this then begs the question, if we have the third person
of the Trinity living in us, and if we have the blood of Jesus

and the second person of the Trinity cleansing us, and if we have the love of God the Father to embrace us, why do we worry? I'm sure every one of us can find different reasons and give different explanations ranging from: "Well, we're just human, so this is how I am, for it runs in my family (hello Damaris), to I don't know, but I know I don't have enough faith.

So today as I'm driving home from the farm, I am consciously making a decision to hold on to worry no more—to let the truth that the one who created me, who died on the cross for me, and who dwells within me, is more than capable of carrying me through all that life brings in my journey, because and only because, He knows my name, and has followed me from my mother's womb till now and unto eternity, because all the days of my life are written in His book.

He knows the beginning to the end. He has a purpose for me. There is a reason why you and I are alive today! Hallelujah! And as I walk in obedience, getting to know more about the Trinity, I can confidently say, "Sin has no more hold on me, and by this today I mean worry, because worry is a sin, right? What an absolute amazing truth!"

Glory hallelujah. Sing and shout. Declare and proclaim. Freedom is ours. Let that sink in, bride of Christ, and rejoice!

Wrestle with God?

When you find yourself in the wrestle of your life and you fight for survival, who do you hang on to? In the book of Genesis, we read the story of Jacob who physically wrestled with God. Latched on to Him. When you don't know what to do, God is fighting for you. It may look like He is fighting us, but He is fighting for our sake.

God wrestles us with one hand and defends us with the other. If we are not disciplined, we are not legitimate. We must refuse to let go. I will not let go until . . . Pain is a sign that God has not given up on us. Must get real with God. When He is asking the question: What is your name? Jacob was renamed and God blessed him there. Jacob stole a blessing but twenty years later when he got real with God . . . He released blessings.

Who are you, Adrianne? Who are you, Damaris? Who are you, Nick? Maria? Ben?

Who are you, Chris and David?

You are you...?

We need to acknowledge our brokenness. I can't bless the mask you put on. Jacob was transformed into Israel. " Own who you are, not for the purpose of staying there, but so I can bless you." Where the spirit of the Lord is, there is freedom. Take the mask off. Let Him see you stark naked in the sense of total surrender.

He already knows, but He waits. Get alone with Him and allow Him to work and bring healing to your wounds, all your shortcomings, addictions, fears, slavery to men, to feelings. Bow before the Lord and let Him do what only He can do—total transformation. His mercy will break the chains—the burden of anxiety and depression. He will meet you in the heaviness.

Jacob, we are told, wrestled with God until dawn. And the bible says that "when the man saw that he did not prevail against Jacob, he touched his hip socket, and his hip was put out of joint" see Genesis 32:25.

Ouch!

And more than that, wow!

Jacob must have been persuasive. Not a quitter. Strong. Insistent. "… I will not let you go, until you bless me...

And while the sun rose, after being bestowed a blessing, the Bible says that he walked away, limping.

I do not know about you, but I can tell you that, I would prefer to limp out of an encounter with God, then miss His blessing.

And you know what? We do not need to ask His name, like Jacob did.

We know Him.

Because He is our Father.

Father's Day, June 18, 2023, Romanian Baptist Church, San Francisco

Sitting in church and looking out the window, the same tree greeted me. Still tall with a full crown dancing in the wind, he whispered, "You back here? It's been a while!"

"Yeah, it has."

"You back to stay?" he seemed to ask.

"No," I whispered. "No," and a flood of emotions overpowered me!

Sitting in the second row, on the piano side, my fingers ran over the clavier for many, many, services. For years, I brought my children into this community with the desire to raise them in the knowledge and fear of our Heavenly Father. I served as the music leader for the youth, for many young generations, including one my children belonged to. First my girl, then my boy, then the choir, and all the time, the collective worship.

It hit me hard to see a new generation sitting in the pews in front of me. They used to be babies not long ago. And now they have facial hair, curly gelled hair, manicures for the girls, and nice smelling cologne for the boys. Lord, You tell us in Your word that we are but a breath. Born in the morning and gone by dusk. Yet in this short span of time on earth, our Father has a calling for each and every one of us. A destiny! Good work for us to walk into.

Turning my eyes on the tree outside, I told him, "You have been here, and saw all the tears that filled so many of my cups. For more years that I care to count, I sat here absent-minded. My thoughts were with him! Wondering where he was and what he was doing. Tears of despair . . . torment of the soul . . . imagination gone wild.

But God, in His goodness and mercy, took me out of this pit, and holding me in His mighty grip is still leading me down paths of righteousness My Heavenly Father was, is, and will always be, with me! Nothing can separate me from His love! He delights in me and desires to give me hope and a good future!

Because if He takes care of the beasts of the field, the plants and trees of the earth, and the birds of the skies, how much more will He care for the ones whom He loved so much that He gave . . . He gave His only son. So, whosoever believes in Him shall not perish, but have everlasting life!

Be strong and courageous. Do not fear or be in dread of them. For it is the Lord your God who goes with you. He will not leave you nor forsake you. It's written on the church's wall from Deuteronomy 31:6.

How fitting. How much I needed to hear this today as I'm fighting so many emotions. As if the tree heard my thoughts he said, "This place though painful, is a place of comfort for you, and will always be. Because it still speaks of a generation gone before you, one that is here today and one to come in the future. You cannot erase the memories as you cannot erase your past. Years spent here with your family, yes, and even with your now not-your-husband anymore.

I know . . . I do, believe me. I know. You will always bask in the amazing ones and will shudder at the bad ones. And that is okay. Because God the Father is writing your history, and yours had to pass through this church you called your own.

You see, he seemed to continue to say you humans are all passing through. And I have watched, and many do! As a witness to time and the greatness of my Creator, I stood and watched through the window, many services. Like a timeless scene, this earth will one day pass away. And I too will join the creation shouting and awaiting the return of the King of Kings and Lord of Lords. For I have been groaning for a long, long time.

You my dear one, go your way. And remember over there, there is a place prepared for those who loved and waited for His return, where there will be no more night, no more tears, and no more pain.

Go my faithful friend. But remember, He will make all things new one day. And when you come into His kingdom, you will again play and sing, but not from the second row on the piano side, but from the heavenly choir of musicians.

Oh, love that will not let me go, I rest my weary soul in Thee. I give Thee back the life I owe. That is the ocean's depths, it's flow. May richer, fuller be! Filled with praises! Oh, you will sing! Go now . . . until then. Just remember! Remember! Remember!

I Said I'm Not Going to Do it, but I Am Now . . . Here it is!

I have chosen purposefully to stay out of the social media platforms, from either Facebook, Instagram, TikTok, Twitter, and the like. I used to be an avid supporter of Facebook. I posted a lot, but I also became engaged in political and religious conversations, and I actually enjoyed it.

It was, if you wish, a way of letting my convictions be known to others. I like a good debate and debating I did.

Until about five years ago, when my personal life took a turn for the worse, and at the insistence of a few people in my life who loved me dearly, I pulled out. It was a much-needed break. It was a time to focus on me, my family, and my issues, without the public being privy to the inside.

Throughout the years, especially the last five years, there were a lot of issues that I would've liked to address in the open, but my commitment to just stay in obscurity for a while was stronger than my desire to be a presence on social media. I promised my family and friends I would not post anything personal, especially pictures, and I kept to my promise.

However, today, my sense of indignation took over my whole being. Watching highlights from the Grammys last night, my blood boiled. For the record, I do not usually watch these shows. I stopped watching them many years ago: the Oscars, the Emmys, the Grammys. Too much display of selfishness, pride, idolatry, confused people full of conceit, blinded by the paparazzi cameras, bragging about their outfits and achievements. The Holy Spirit convinced me that this should not be the focus and interest of a child of God. So I gave it up and I can tell you honestly, I don't miss it!

But reading the highlights from the 2023 Grammys, I decided to take to the Facebook Meta platform and say: "We are living in the end of times when the debauchery of people has reached an all-time high." I can almost hear that Father telling the Son and Holy Spirit: "Let's go down and mess up their plans." Reminiscing about the Tower of Babel story in the Old Testament, it almost calls for an intervention like that.

Except this time, the intervention will be much more grand, more amazing and worthy of all the newspapers and news channels. When Christ comes to take up His bride, the people left behind will be bewildered. So here is my trumpet sound, the sound of alarm for the bride of Christ: When you see these things happening, lift up your heads and your hearts because your redemption is near. It's right at the door.

The performance of the song "Unholy" last night, left me nauseous. The shameless parade of sin applauded by everybody in the audience, and the mention of the word God and their success attributed to Him by some artists almost made me choke. Yes, I can choke back tears and I can wail in distress for those whom I love and are not walking with the Lord today.

I want to scream from the top of my lungs for the bride of Christ to purify herself—to refuse to endorse, listen, and promote even so-called Christian artists. I was astonished to see Maverick City receiving their award. "I listen to their music," I said to myself, "and now they are in that room, full of Satan worshippers, receiving their accolades and golden statue."

Nope, no more, I will not listen to their music again! They

have to preach what they are singing. They have to live the way they identify themselves as Christian artists. I'm afraid, if not, they will hear those hateful words spoken by Christ himself: "Depart from me . . . I never knew you."

My prayer for myself, for my friends, for my family, and or all the people that I love and care about, is that we purify ourselves, that we use discernment and wisdom to know what to allow to come into our eyes and ears, from festivals, musicals, movies, shows, and any kind of entertainment.

And yes, even Christian platforms where sadly, people pose as wolves in sheep's clothing: lukewarm, deceiving, self-promoting, gospel diluting, sin differing, culture inclusive, people pleasing, ear tacklers, false teachers, and preachers.

Lord, in the name of Jesus, I pray for the body of Christ to stay vigilant. To watch and pray, to believe and to spread the good news of the gospel, to love the unloved and await the wonderful day when at the sound of the trumpet, all of us who are alive will be caught up in the air to meet Christ. Oh, what a glorious day it would be. Until then, keep up the good faith and the good work, Christians.

HEALTH SCARES,
BUT MUCH NEEDED DETOURS

Me and My Stone

A stone of remembrance, a stone rolled away, a stone picked up to be cast on someone who was worthy of death, in some of the public squares of ancient Israel. A stone which was ready to praise if the people of God would not have—a stepping stone, a corner stone, *the* corner stone. Hmm . . . a stone that Jesus could've turned into bread, a sling, and five stones, one which killed the giant, a tombstone, a milestone, and, a gallbladder stone.

Up until a few months ago, I did not know that I had a gallbladder. You might say, "C'mon, you are a nurse. Surely you knew you had one?" to which I would answer, "I did not know I had a malfunctioning one, one that was rebelling and betraying me by forming stones."

When the pain in my abdomen was too much to bear and not responding to the usual remedies, I called my doctor. She wanted me to come in. Ah, I do not like to go and see them—not as a patient anyway, but as a fellow medical professional, but I went in anyway. Bloodwork followed and an order for an ultrasound. And low and behold, it showed that I have a 1.9 cm gallbladder stone.

Betrayer! That is how I felt towards the tiny little organ whose job is to store bile which in turn is being used for the digestion of food, primarily fats. But instead of doing its job, it decided to form cholesterol stones. So far only one, but a "boulder," the size of a walnut! I was not happy, and I named the stone Judah. Maybe I should have named the gallbladder, but no matter. I had inside of me something that did not belong there, and it caused me a whole lot of pain.

I then went to talk to a surgeon, and it was decided that I would do this laparoscopically, an outpatient procedure. I told her that I would not go to the emergency room unless I was dying in pain. No, I had no desire to be impatient though I came close to doing it a few times, but I persevered. The attacks are gruesome and are comparable to labor pains. No fun at all, especially since when a mother is in labor, at least she knows that she will get to see her baby. It felt like it was a birthing, but a stone?

"Judah, had to go!" I started to make jokes about him (yes, I had decided it was a male), because only they, can inflict so much pain into us, the female gender. Anyone with me? I would then say, "I am taking my stone to the store and then to my parent's house," or "My stone and I are going to church, and I would proceed to tell him to behave and that I do not have time for pain." Kind of reminds me of Carly Simon's song "Haven't Got Time for the Pain." I was told I am funny—I am trying.

I shared with some of my church friends about Judah and the joke that he perpetuated was: Is he still with you? How is Judah doing? I know it might sound strange to some of you, but my mind works this way. My parents and siblings think that I am strange, to which I always reply, "I was born this way, and no I am not making any reference to Lady Gaga's song. No, no. But I continued, "One in eight came out to be the weirdo. Oh well. Glad the rest of you are normal."

I had to reschedule the surgery once because of some family business, but I have to tell you that it was getting pretty hard to keep him. In the Bible, in the Gospel of John, when Judah betrayed the Lord, Jesus told him this: "What you have to do, do fast." I wish I could rid myself of my Judah, fast, but I was about to discover just a few weeks later that he was going to stay longer.

Awaiting my surgery scheduled for the beginning of October, I started to not feel well—severe exhaustion and running out of steam. I did not want to think it was anything serious. Who wants to, unless you are a hypo? So, I put it out of my mind, but sadly, it was putting me out of my breath.

My doctor asked me to go to the emergency room. I declined, initially. "Can this be done as an outpatient procedure?"

"No," she said. "Not enough time." So last Sunday morning after church, dressed in my church garb, I walked into the ER.

"Are you here for yourself?"

Yes," I said. "But not by my own will. My doctor forced me."

"What seems to be the problem? she continued, looking at me kind of strange.

"I am short of breath with any exertion."

"Sign here, and here, and here."

What followed was the usual ER triage, followed very quickly by the words: "You need to be admitted."

"What? I came to be here for just two hours and then go home."

"Sorry, but it looks like you have an acute coronary syndrome."

"What? No, no, no. Are you talking to me? Are you sure you don't have the wrong patient?"

"Yes. You are positive for heart ischemia."

Then like a bomb had hit, my mind reeled. No, Lord. First Judah, now this? But in a matter of a few hours, I was in the ambulance being transferred to the cardiac thoracic unit of the hospital located in the next town.

"Well, Judah," I said. "It looks like you and I are going to bond some more. It looks like I now have to take care of Honor, my heart, who is sick and needs my total attention. You have to promise me you will stay calm and not disturb me. I will be busy for a while. Do you understand?"

And to my surprise.... no answer came! To be continued

From the Cardiac Unit . . . with Love

Music is playing softly in my hospital room and in a moment of total surrender, I know He is here. His presence is undeniable. Tears flow freely and my gown is soaking in them gladly. Lord, I know you have a plan and I know I am here for a reason. This is the chorus I had my daughter repeat for herself for the last few months and this will be the same chorus I will sing for my life. I was supposed to be in Romania but postponed my trip due to Judah, my gallbladder stone, and now this!

I am not unaware of the enemy's schemes. He wanted me dead many times and it seems he is not giving up. But God... Being in a teaching hospital I got to meet a lot of doctors. And being the way that I am, I loved to talk to them. The fellow who is above the residents came in first. They were all so nice to me, maybe because I am one of their own. We went over my history and the plan, and then I asked, "Do you believe in God? And to my surprise, the answer was, "No."

I said to the fellow, "You must have seen and surely you know how amazing this body works, but you don't believe in an intelligent design?"

"I think evolution is what caused it all," he replied. He then told me that he came from a Hindi background but his father was a strong Christian.

"And it didn't pass down to you?" I asked.

"No, it did not," was his reply. And I thought to myself, you just don't know how many prayers he lifted up on your behalf. You never know what God can do.

Then in walks Dr. Fatima, one of the residents. Small-framed with beautiful dark curly hair, her face was covered by a mask. I start telling her the story of why I came to the hospital. I told her that I took my stone to church and afterwards, we had to come here due to my shortness of breath. She giggled when I told her that I had named my gallstone Judah.

"What are you going to name your heart?" she asked

"I have not though about it, I said," but I am taking that as my homework."

She was simply delightful. She expressed empathy for what happened to me and I told her I was relying on my faith to get me through this. She told me she is a Muslim and believes too. Lord, the children of Ishmael are many, but their convictions are sadly not biblical. First an atheist, now a Muslim. I am taking it all in.

Not long after, I was visited by another resident, Dr. Anderson. Young and handsome, he said to me, "You are very popular."

"I love it," I said, and proceeded to answer more questions.

Later, by myself in my room when all the phone conversations ceased for a minute, I allowed myself to look inside and see my heart. Battered from years of emotional pain, battered by self-neglect and genetics which sadly cannot be tampered with, she continues to pump and keep up with all that is being thrown at her, though tired at times.

I whispered, "Honor, you have served me well. Through good and bad times, not like a partner, but like a faithful friend. I named you Honor because like your name, you have honored me with your faithful beat. One hundred thousand times per day you have been pumping my blood, each day, 365 days a year for fifty-six years. You have not tired. You faithfully did your job with all diligence. Can I tell you that I am honored? Can I tell you that I am thankful? And can I tell you that I am grateful? Yes, I am, Honor. Because you have not only honored me, but the One who created you. When He formed you in the secret, intricately woven in my mother's womb, you started to beat so very early into my existence. And you have not stopped since, though you've tired a bit lately and I do understand.

"And I am honored to have you, Honor. You have served me well. Now you know that we are about to embark on this new journey. They told me they will give you new beating power, Honor, so you will not tire so easily. Can you imagine that? Would you like that? Because tomorrow you and I will walk into this together. We will hold tight to one another for dear life. And no matter how hard, we will overcome this."

"I did not tattoo 'Overcomer' on my wrist for nothing! And we will worship Him together. Oh, how I love Him. I do, Honor. I do. He deserves all the praise. But then, you know that don't you? Because by serving me, you have honored Him! And for this, I am humbled."

ABOOKS

ALIVE Book Publishing and ALIVE Publishing Group
are imprints of Advanced Publishing LLC,
3200 A Danville Blvd., Suite 204, Alamo, California 94507

925.837.7303
alivebookpublishing.com